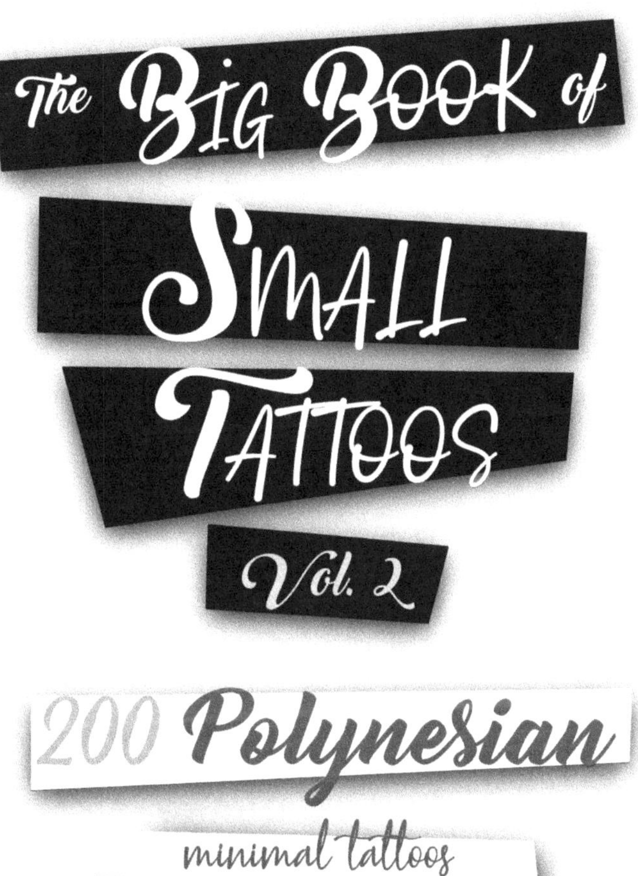

TattooTribes

2021

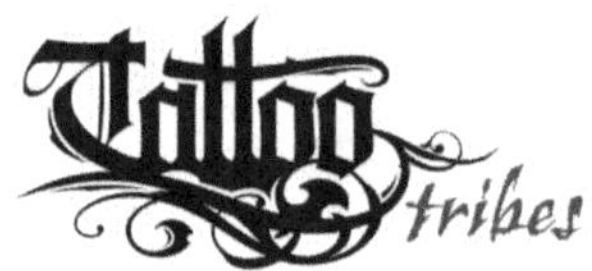

TattooTribes Ed.
© 2021 Roberto Gemori.

ISBN-13: 978-88-942056-2-6

ISBN-10: 88-942056-2-2

All original images by TattooTribes.

Contents

This volume was inspired by our love for Polynesia and its tattoos and cultures. Each small to minimal design is a statement, embodying an aspect or trait from the Pacific Islands and carrying a memory of palm trees, sun, thriving ocean life, and sandy beaches.

Enjoy.

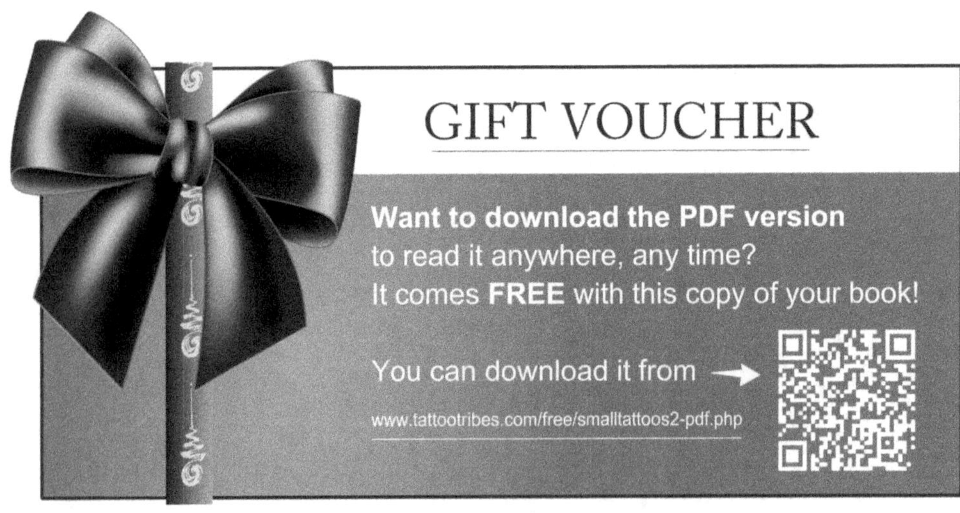
GIFT VOUCHER

Want to download the PDF version
to read it anywhere, any time?
It comes FREE with this copy of your book!

You can download it from →

www.tattootribes.com/free/smalltattoos2-pdf.php

Preface

The Big Book of Small Tattoos is a project by TattooTribes that aims at bringing a new perspective on the concept of small tattoos.

The underlying idea, which is shared throughout the whole work of our artists, is that small tattoos can be highly meaningful and original despite their small size: the significance of a tattoo is not decided by its size, and even the smallest design can carry a great meaning.

Based on these premises, we knew that we wouldn't have been true to our mission if we simply collected existing designs from the web or wherever, and so we started this original project that will feature in the end over 3,000 small and meaningful designs never published before.

Here's why this book, and all the others in this series, are unique: every and each tattoo has been designed specifically for these books. They didn't exist before, and they can't be found anywhere else.

Mantas, turtles, sharks, whales, seashells, fish hooks, tropical flowers, waves, guardian spirits, suns, and palm trees—all of them and many more found their way into this book, as they immediately come to mind when thinking about Polynesia.

Some designs are very simple; others are made by joining smaller, basic elements from Polynesian tattoos, creating new designs that inherit their meanings from the symbols that compose them.

Since the basic elements and symbols of Polynesian tattoos are too many to fit into this book (we actually published two bigger volumes specifically dedicated to them, *The*

Polynesian Tattoo Handbook 1 and 2), the section at the end of this book explains only the meanings of the main elements, as a quick reference to what each design symbolizes.

It's amazing to see that, using the proper symbols, stories can be told and weaved within a Polynesian tattoo, and if you feel curious about how it's done and would like to know more, we also publish monthly articles about Polynesian tattoo symbols, history, and meanings (the five main styles are Samoan, Marquesan, Tahitian, Maori, and Hawaiian). They are free to read and download as PDF cards from

https://www.polynesiantattoosymbols.com/wiki.html

By the way, at the time of this writing, *The Polynesian Tattoo Handbook Volume 1* turned ten years old and we are leaving it free to download to celebrate it with you. Check the link to see if it still is (it will eventually be complimentary to Volume 2 for some more time, and then go back to normal price).

We hope you'll enjoy this book, breathing the spirit of Polynesia from its pages and possibly, who knows, showing it on your own skin and in your heart!

Themes quick index

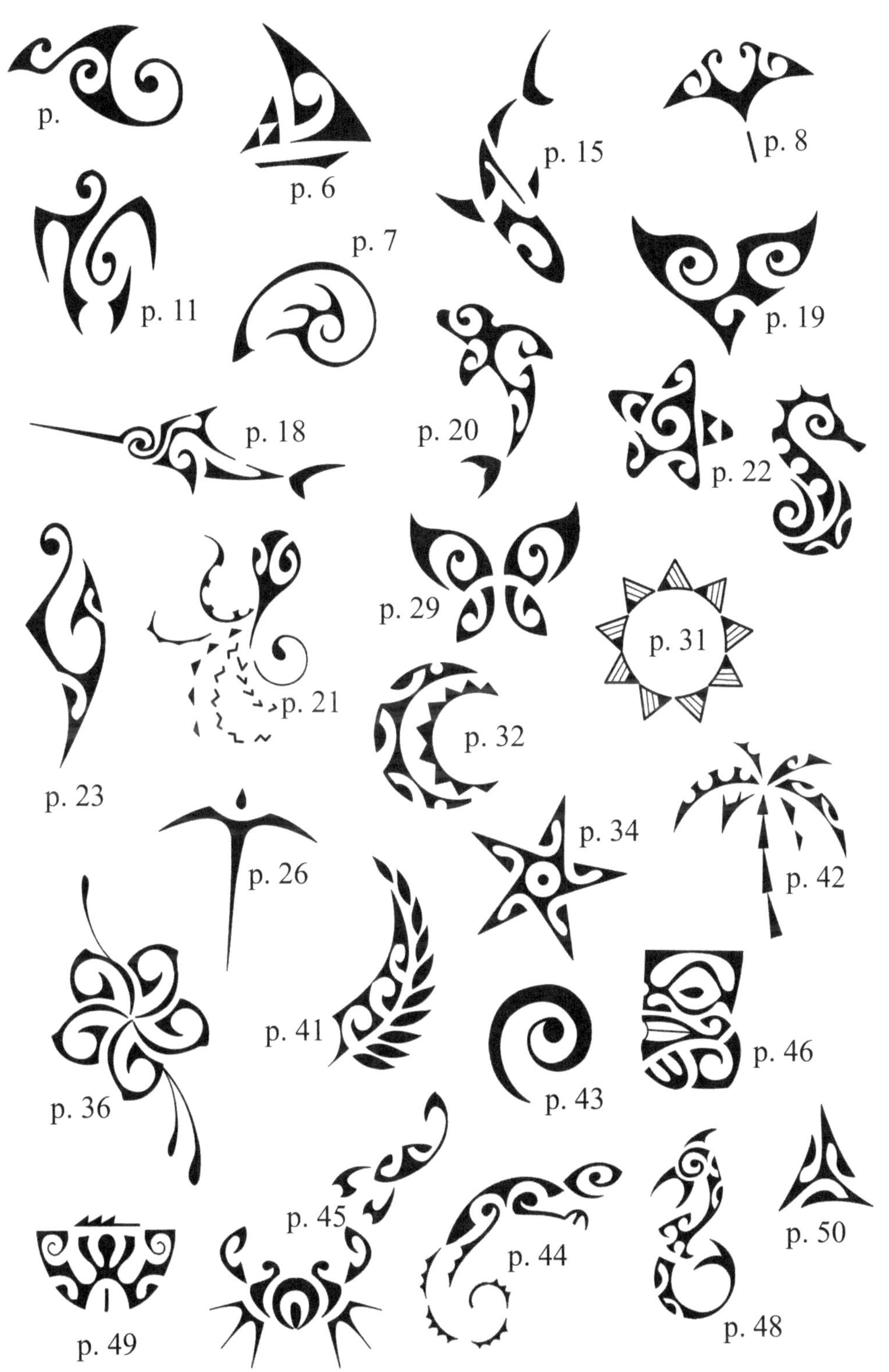

Water

Water-related designs make the greatest part of this book, and it's no surprise since Polynesia is spread across over 165 million square kilometers of ocean. Turtles, mantas, sharks— they were a constant presence in the life of Polynesian people and in their tattoos.

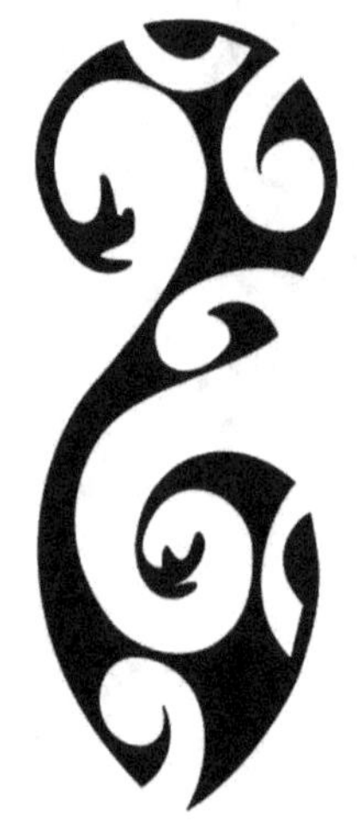

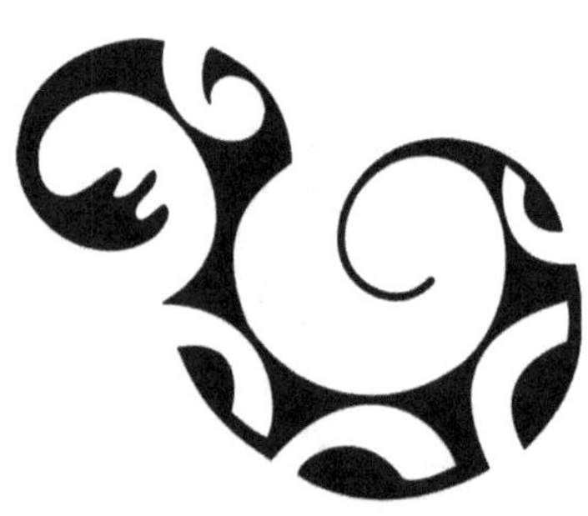

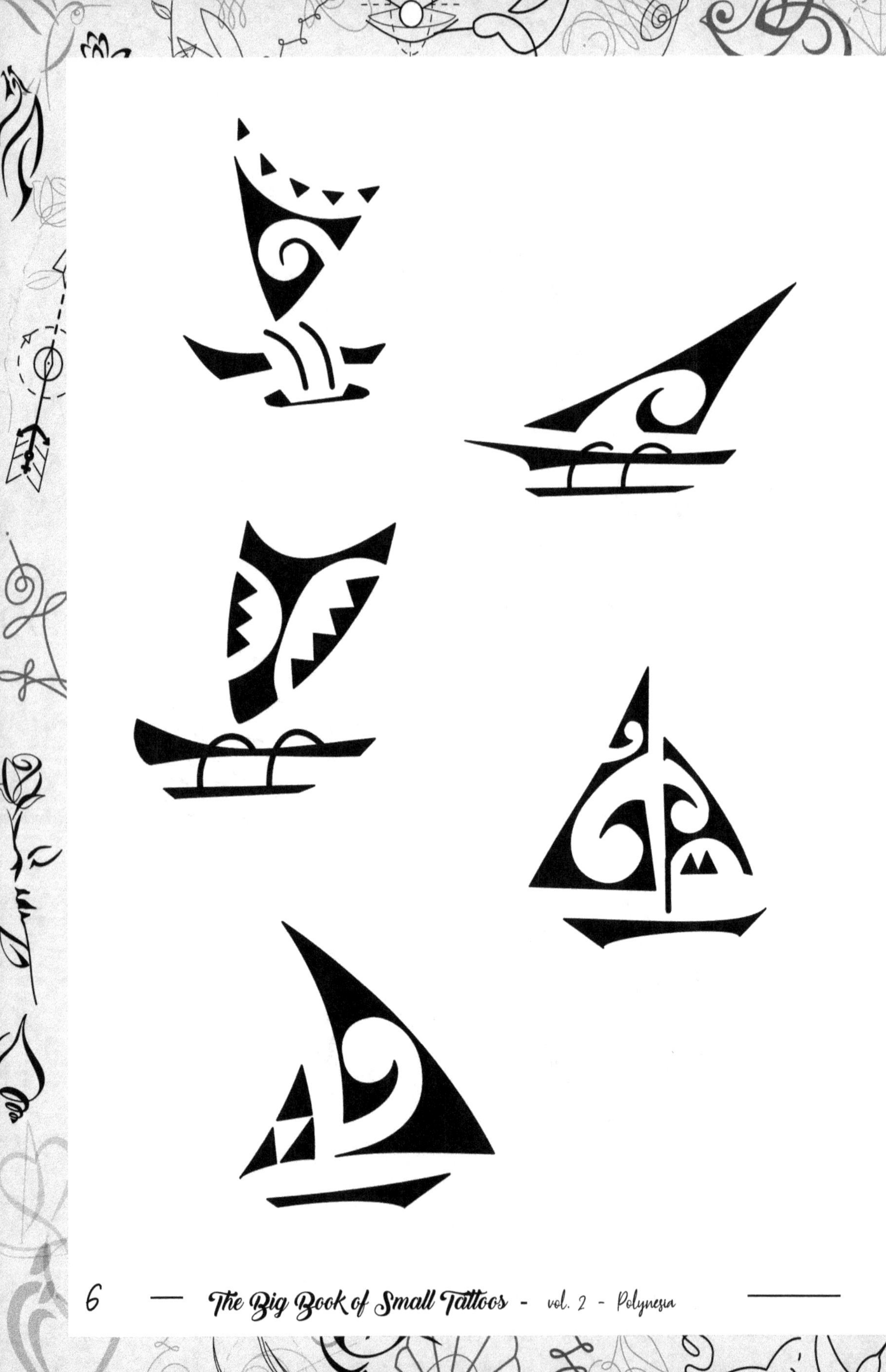

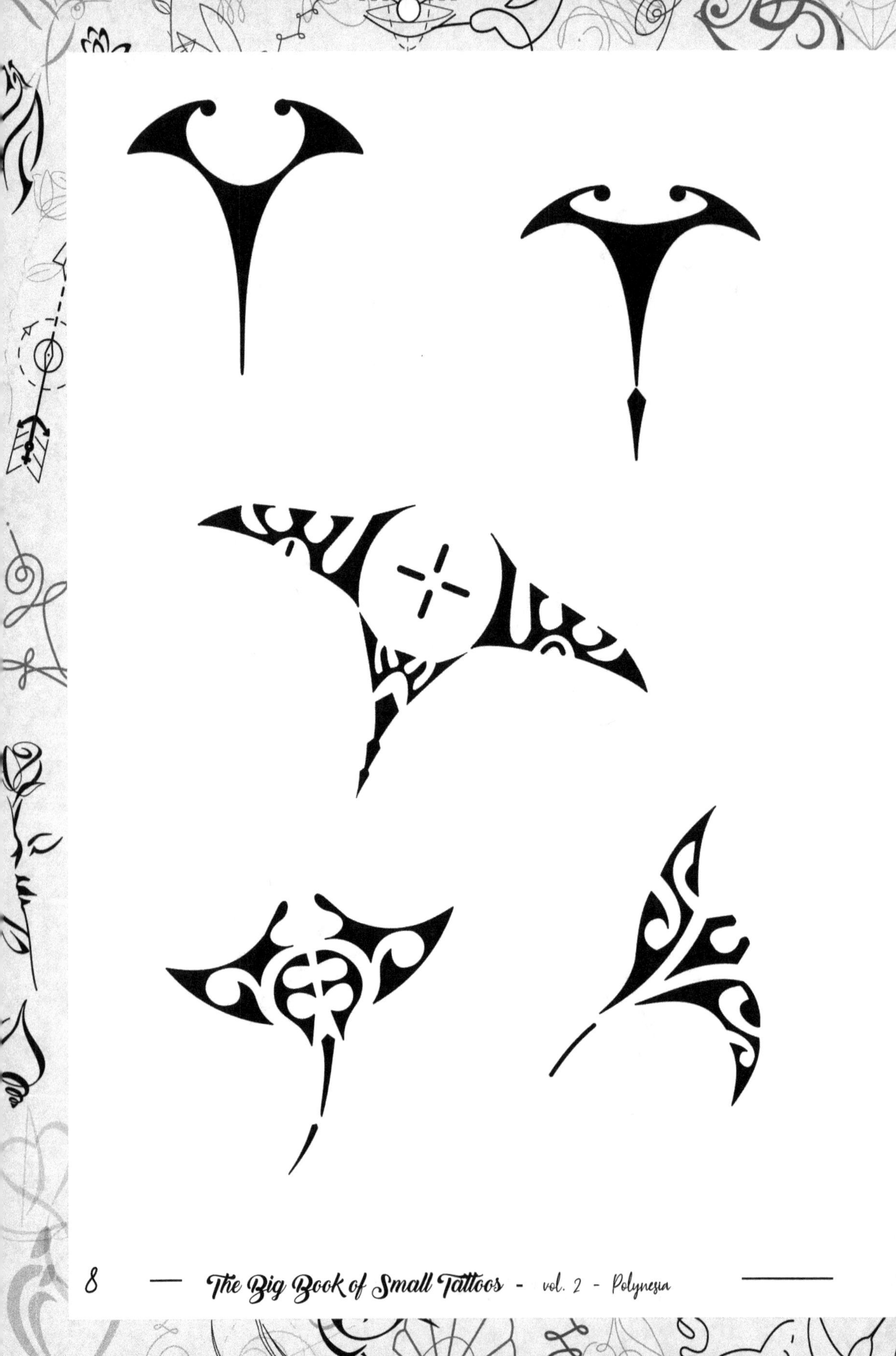

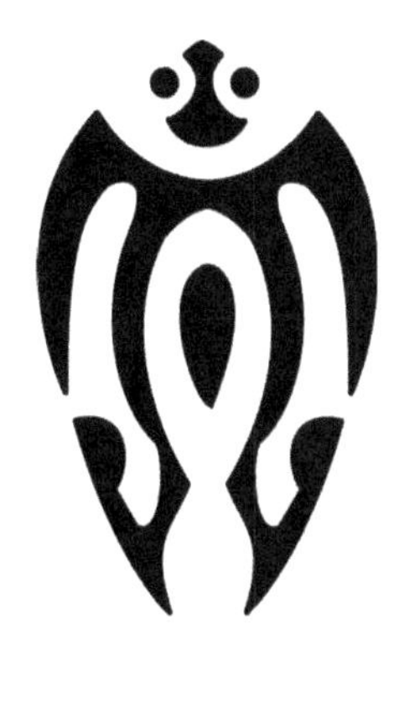

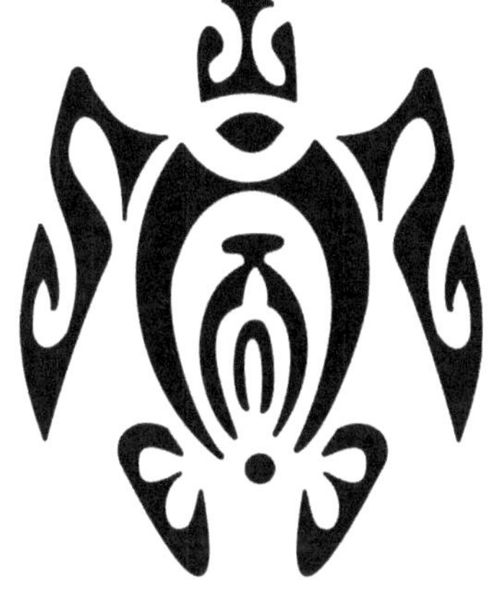

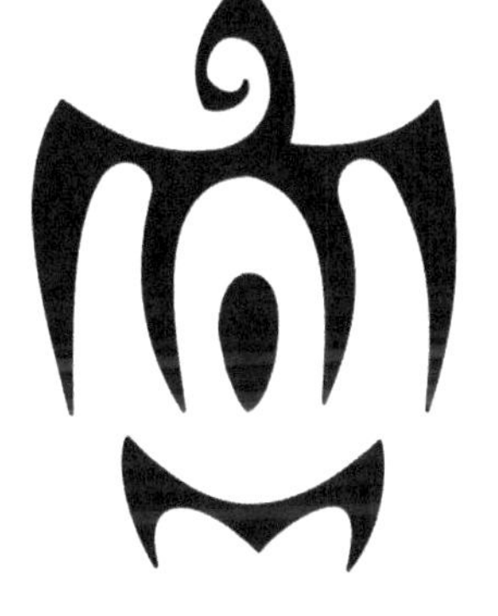

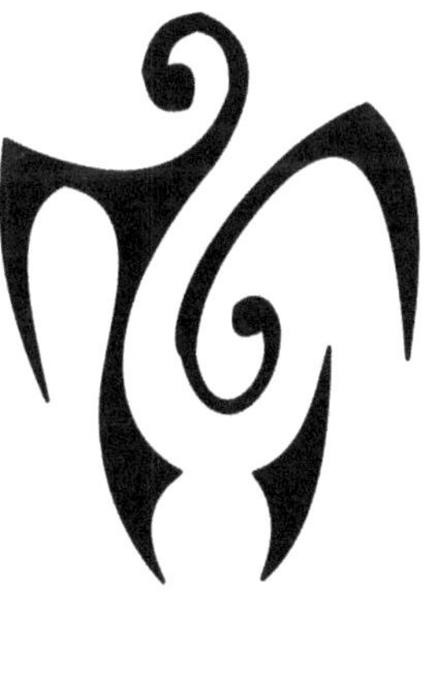

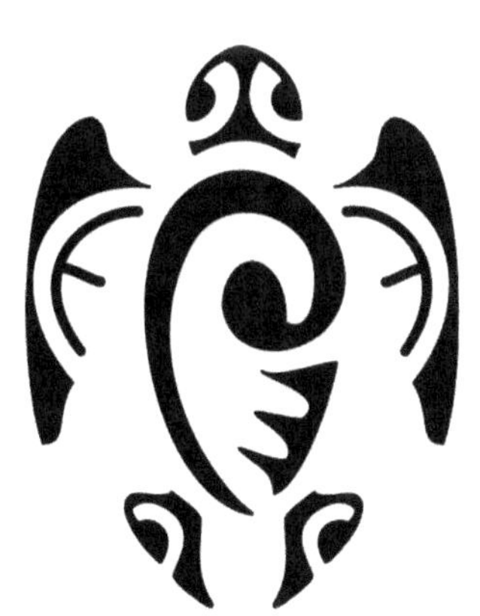

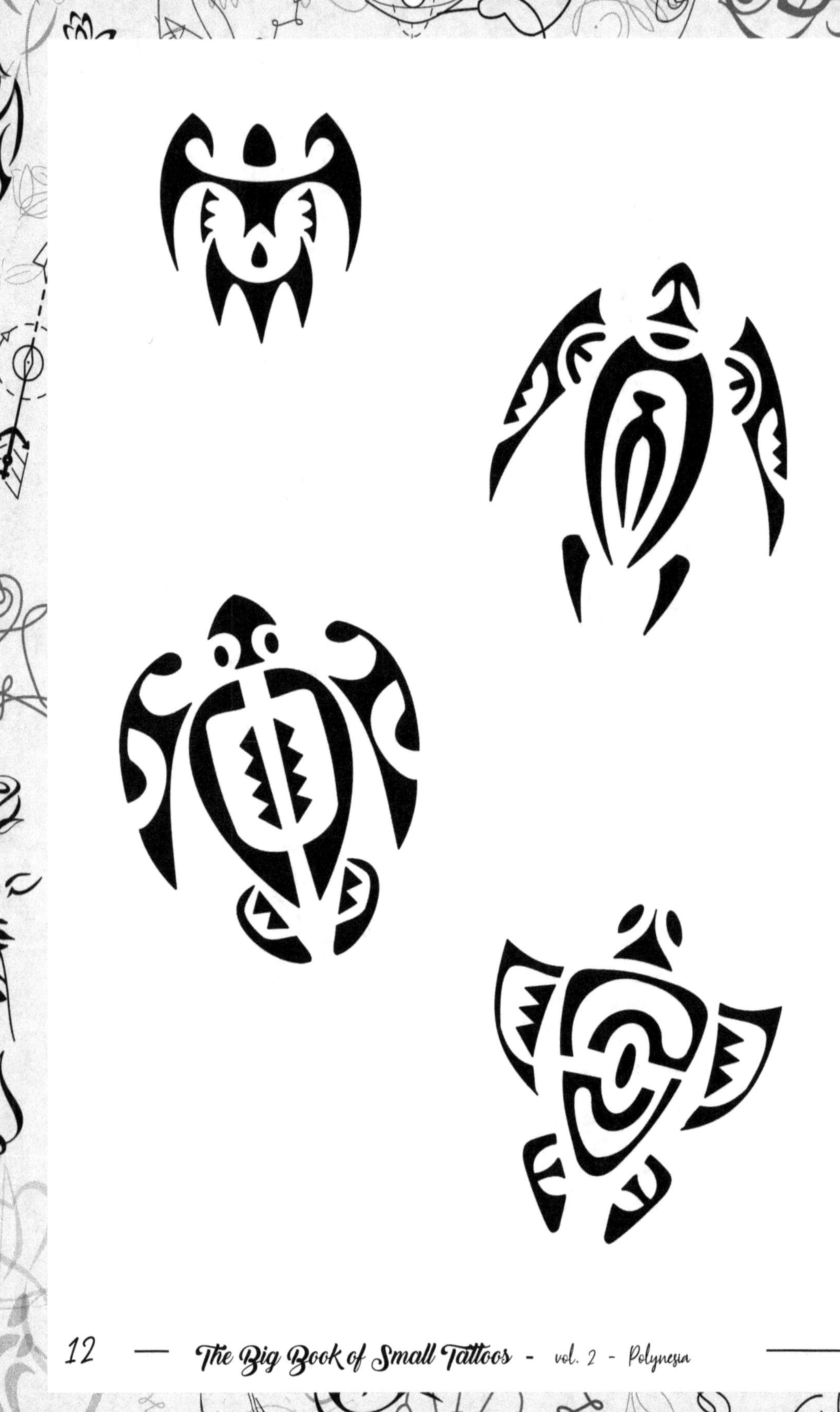

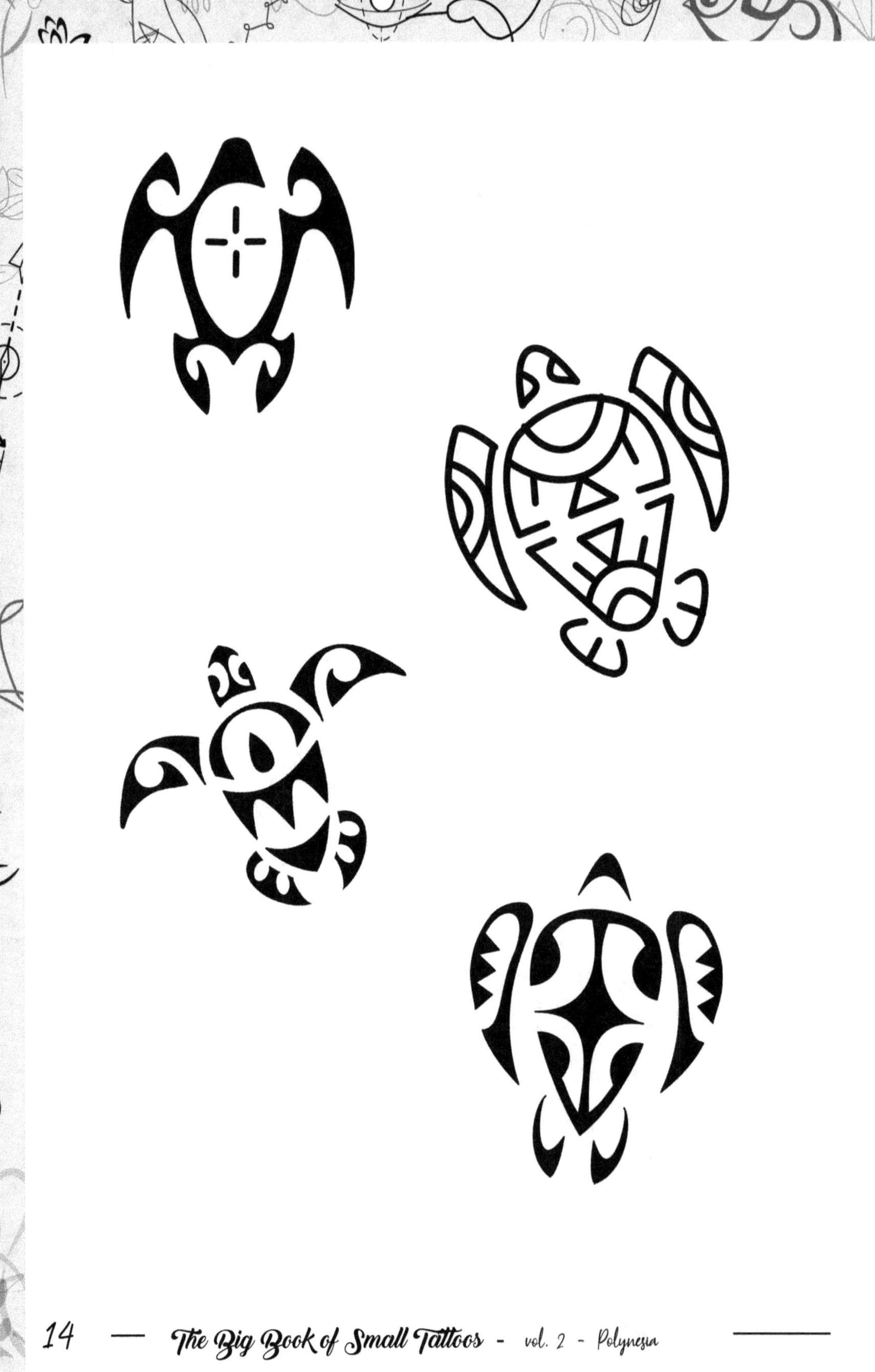

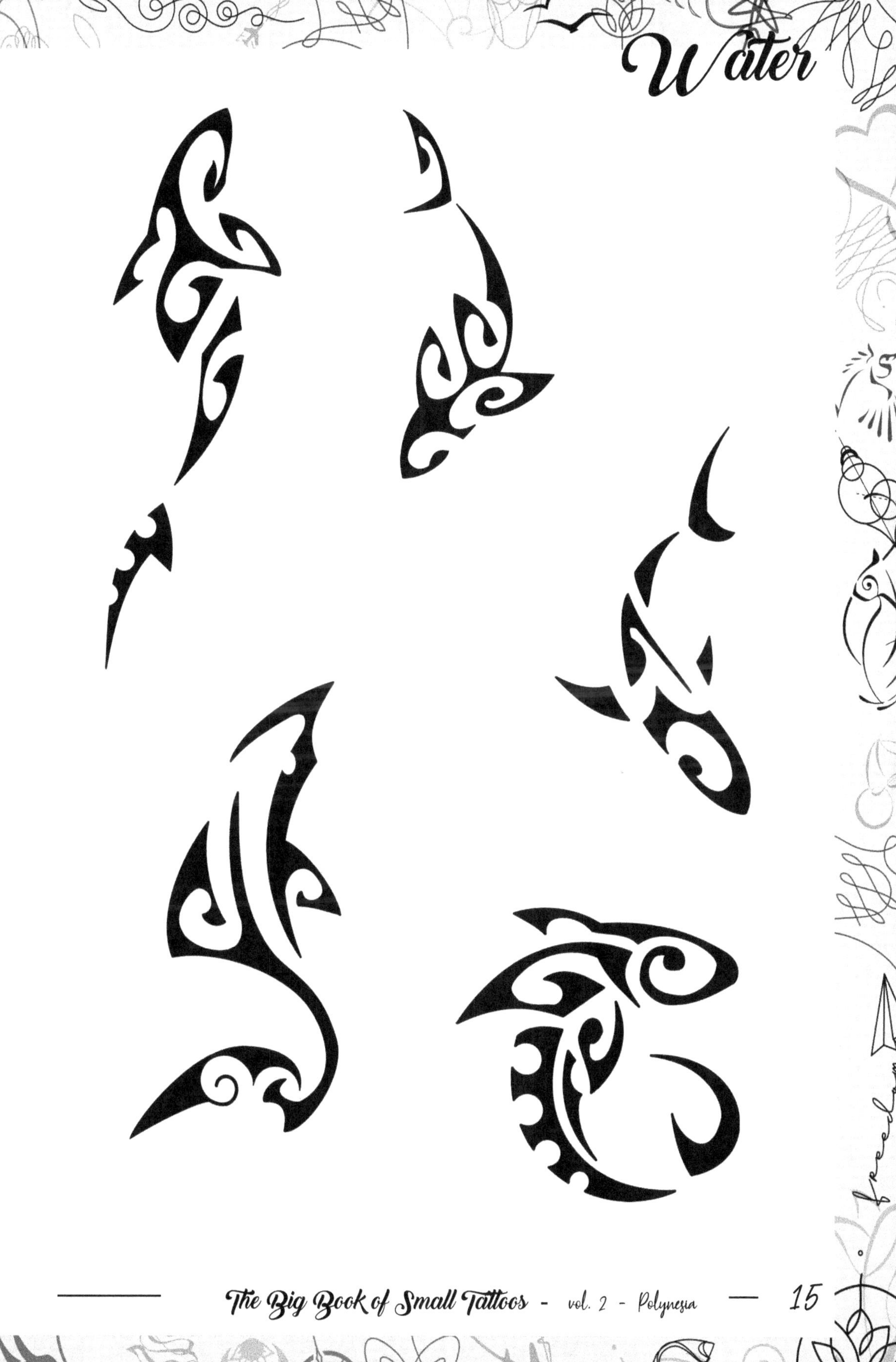

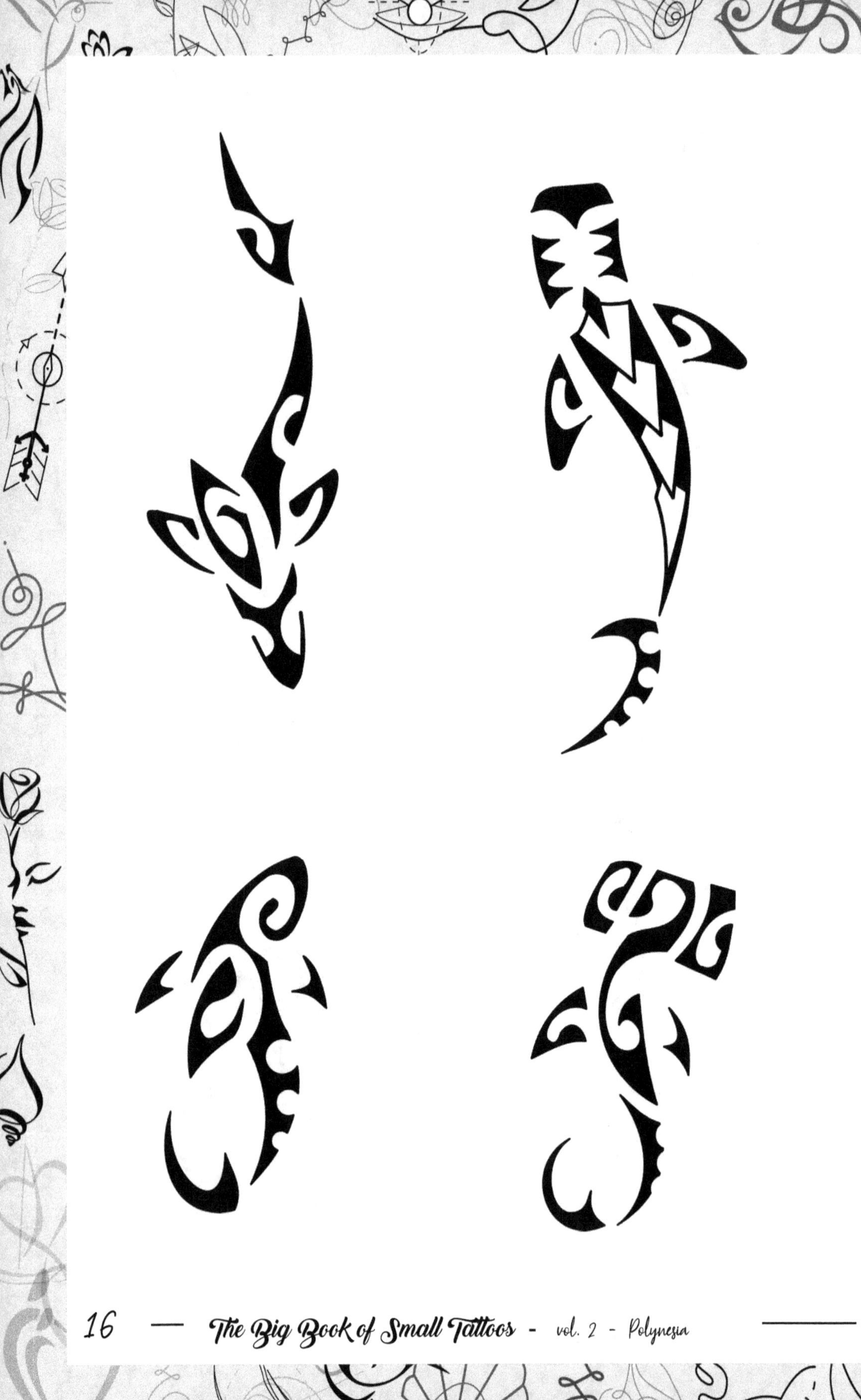

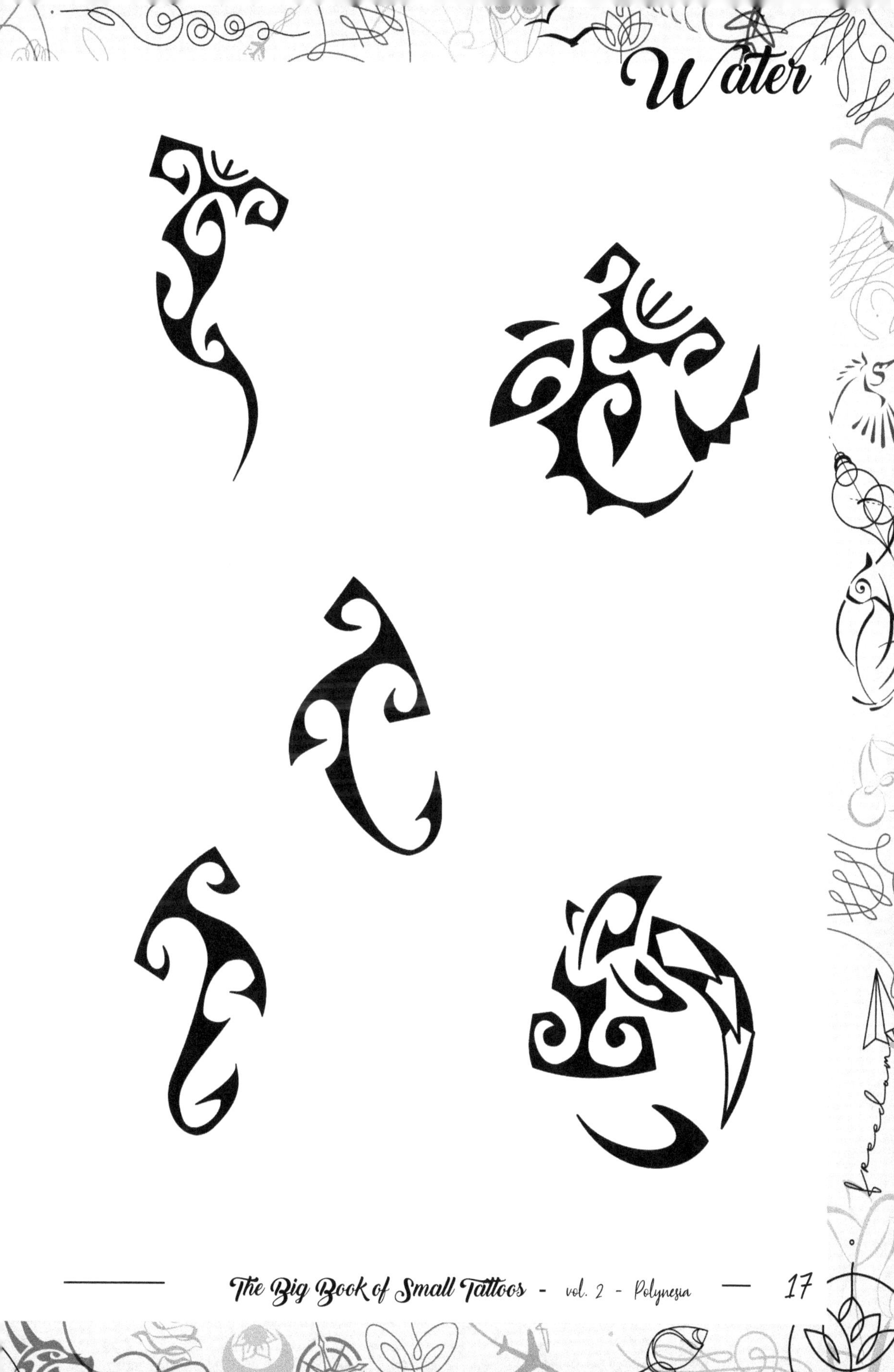

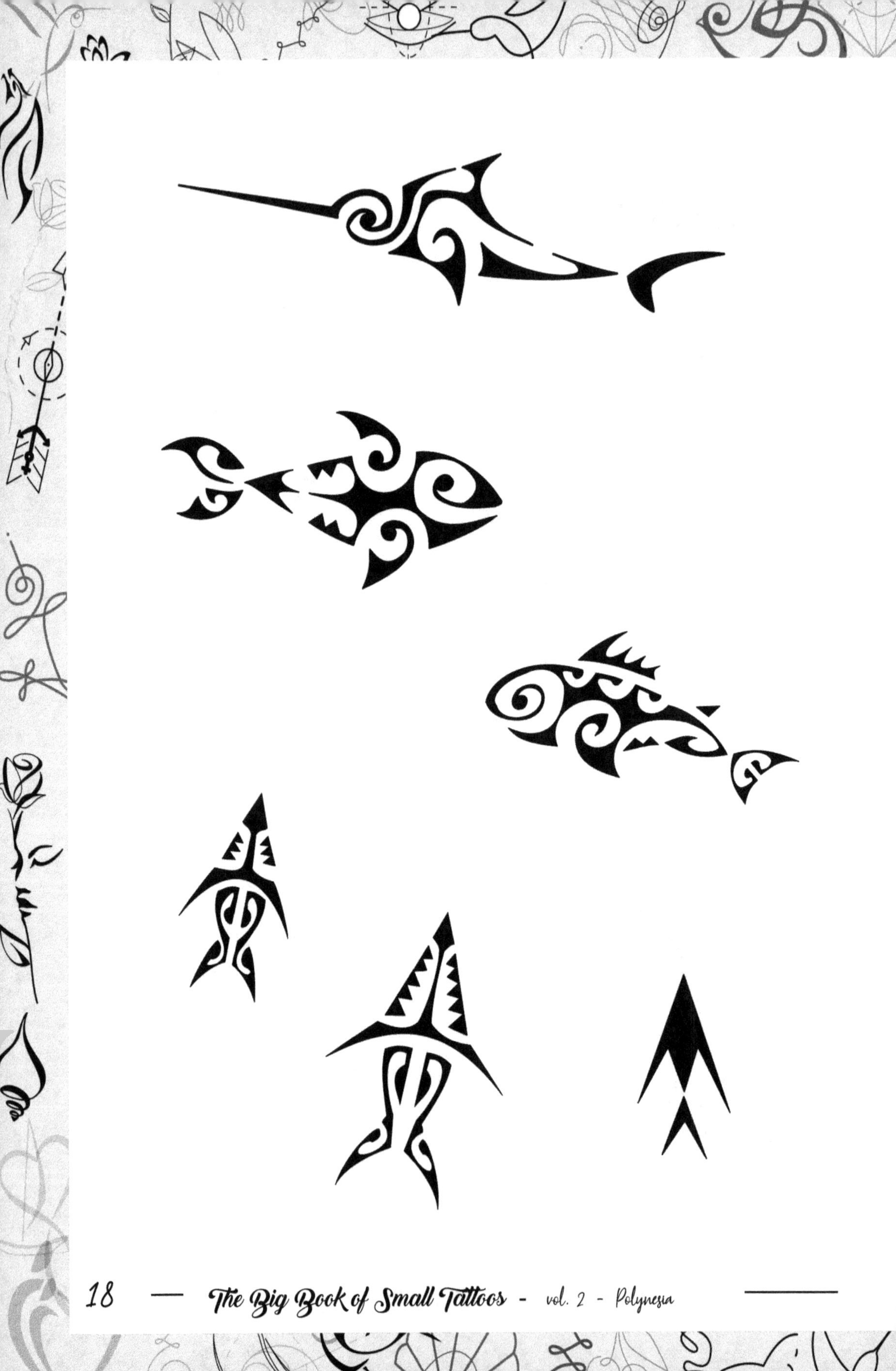

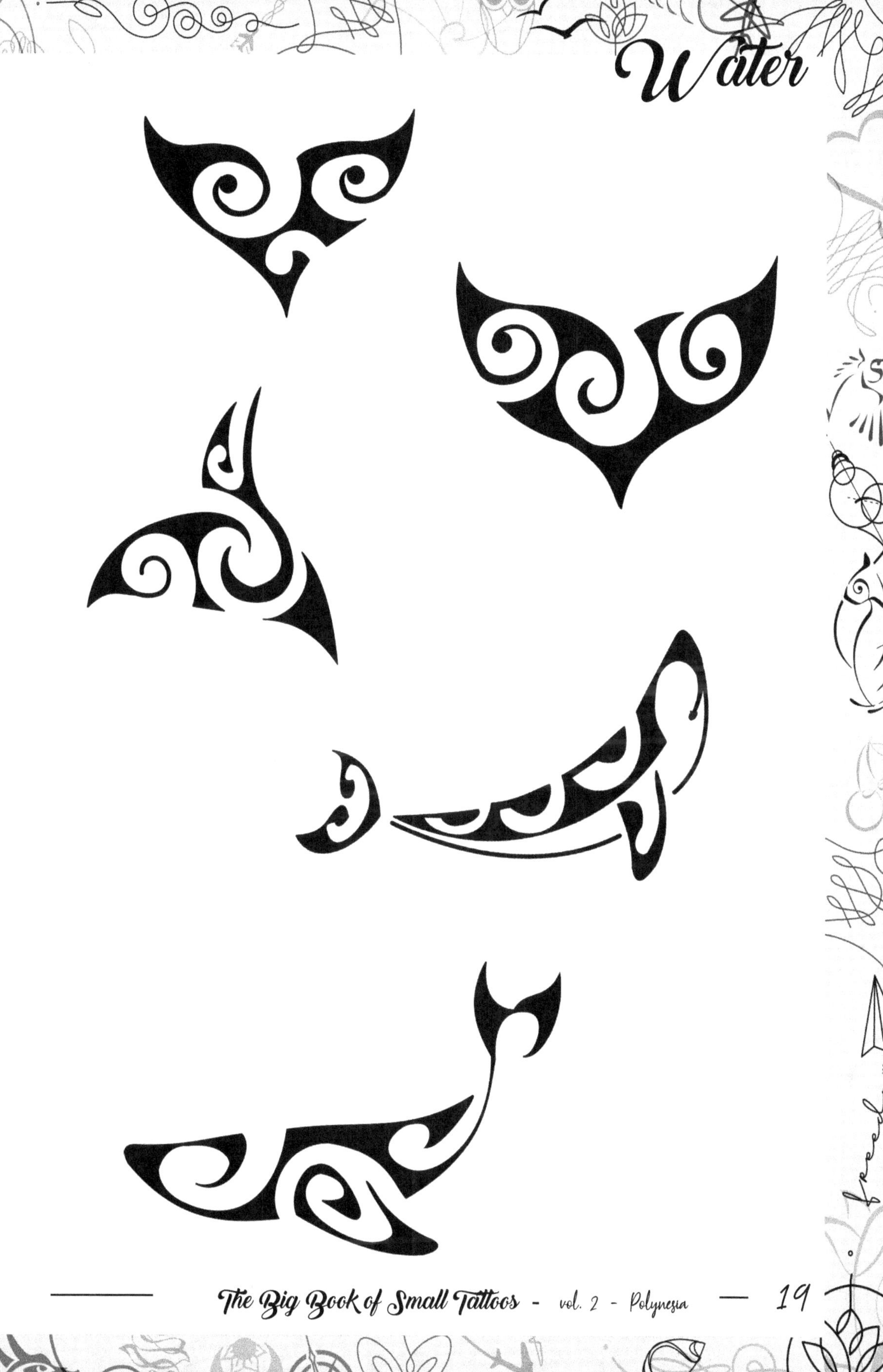

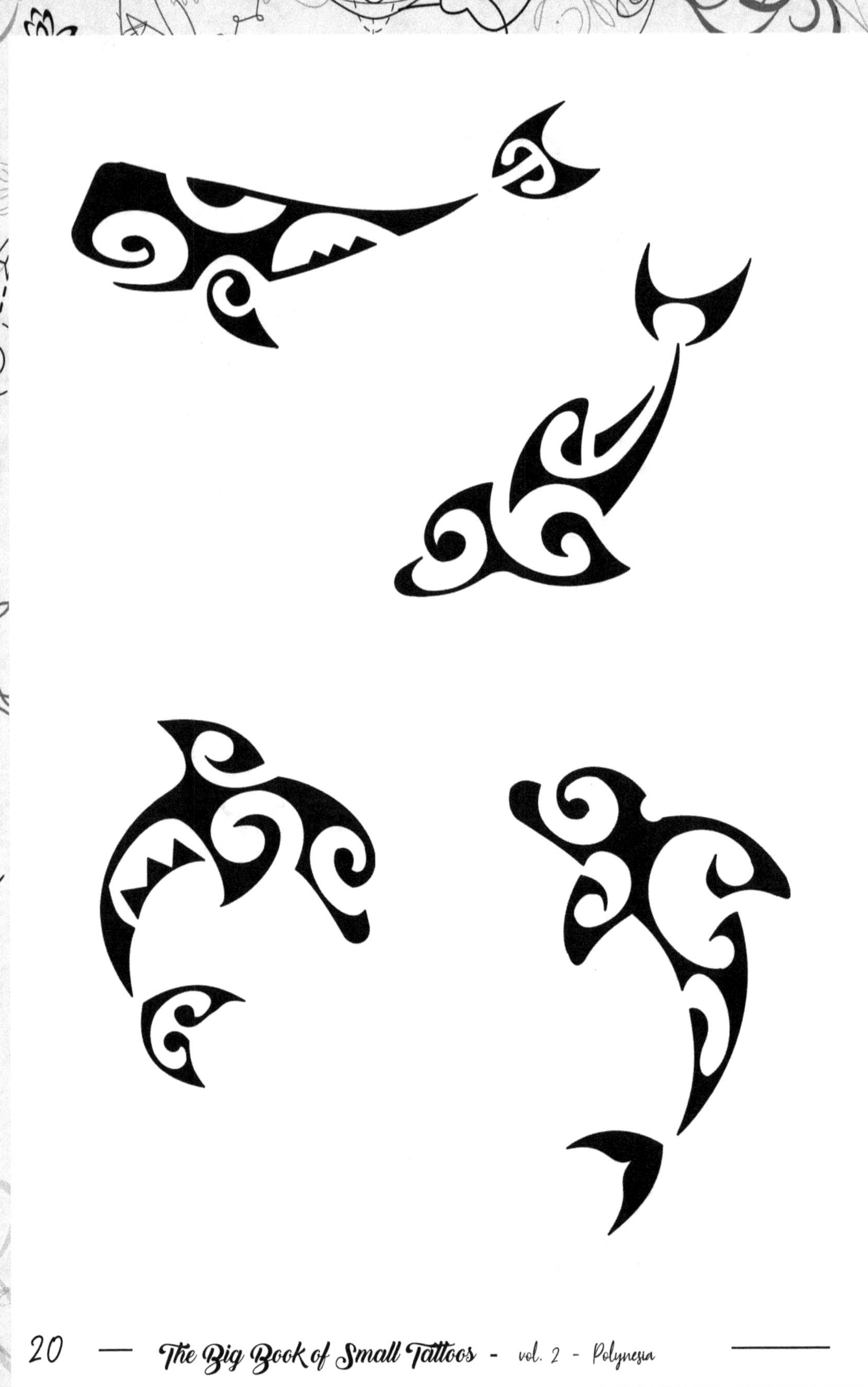

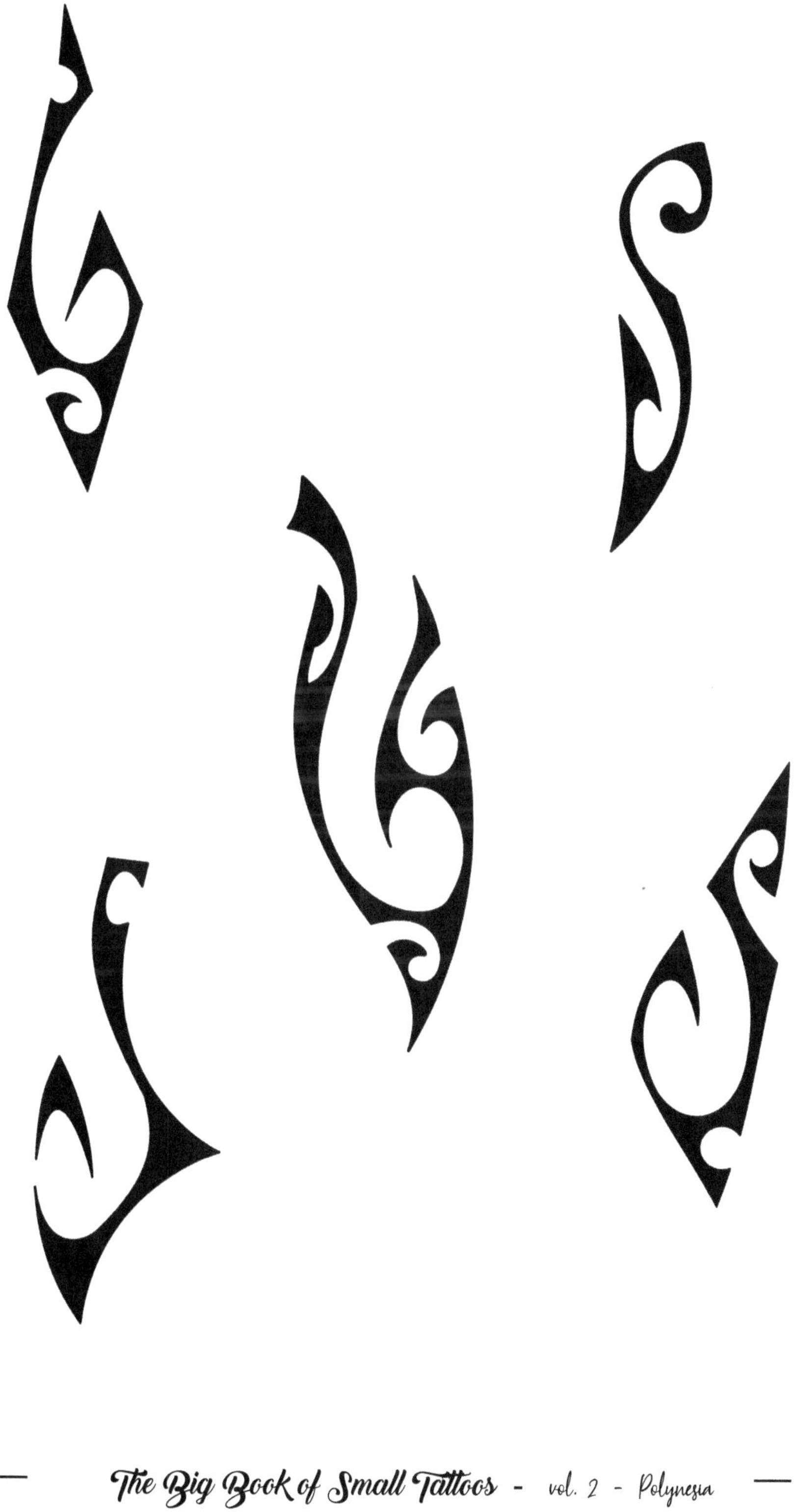

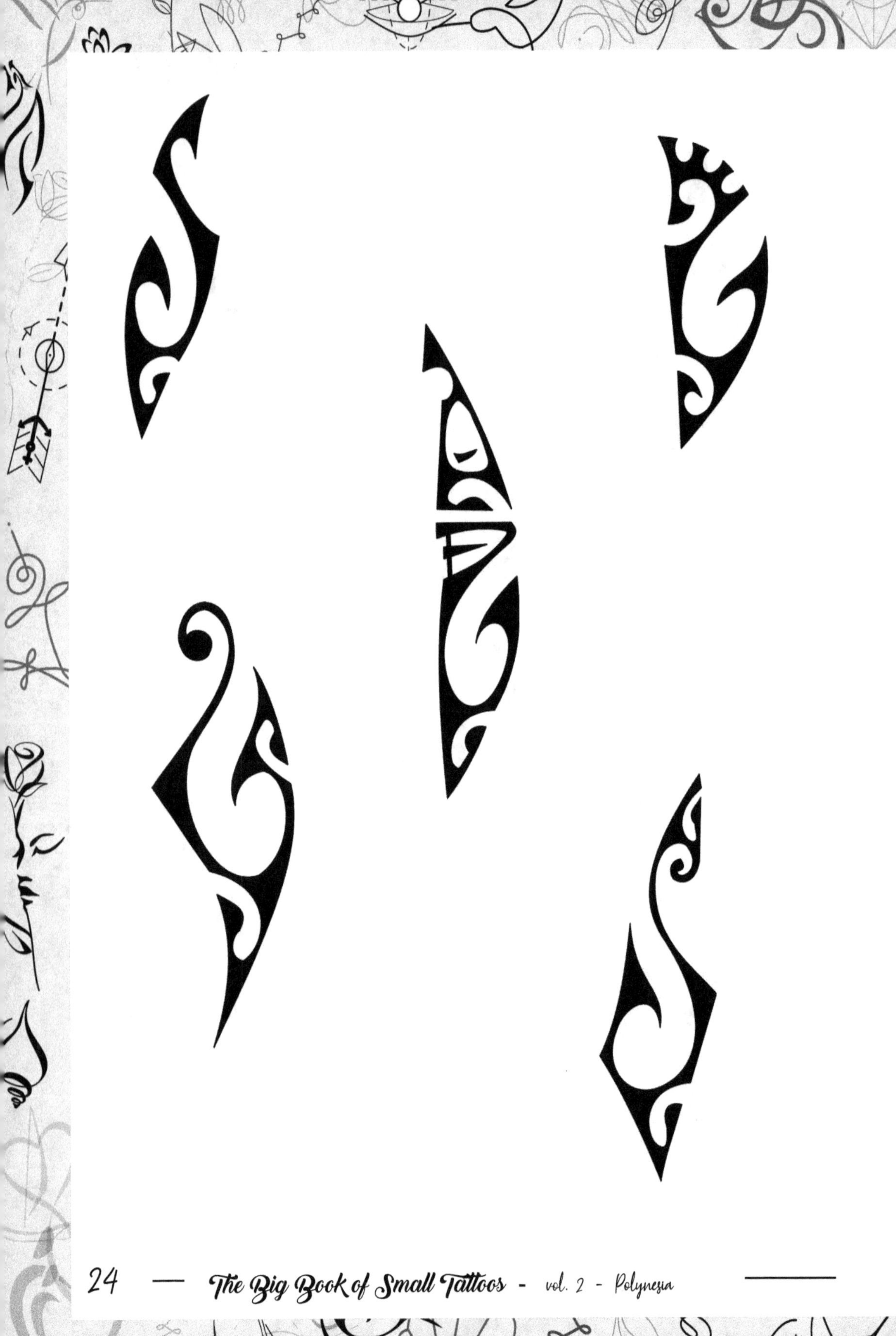

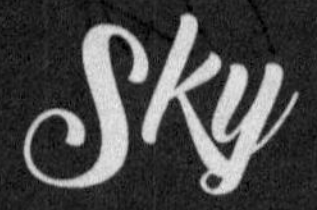

Sky

Polynesian navigators always looked at the sky for guidance and for hints on the path to follow on their voyages from one island to another: stars, winds, clouds, migratory patterns of birds—they all hold valuable information to those who can read it.

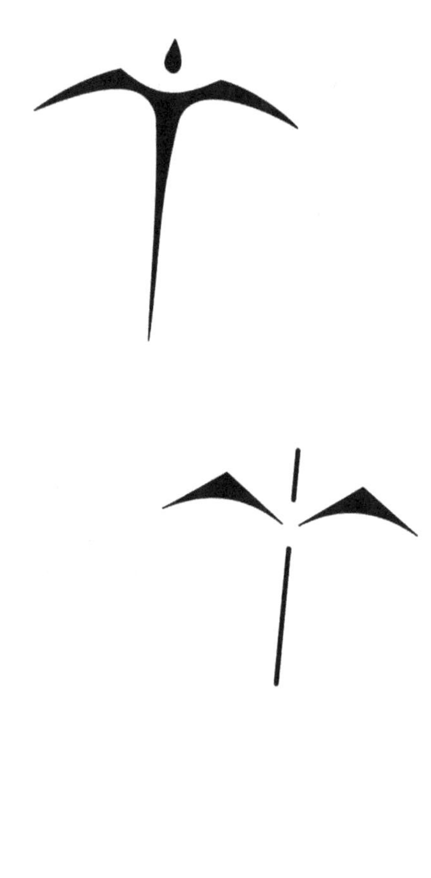

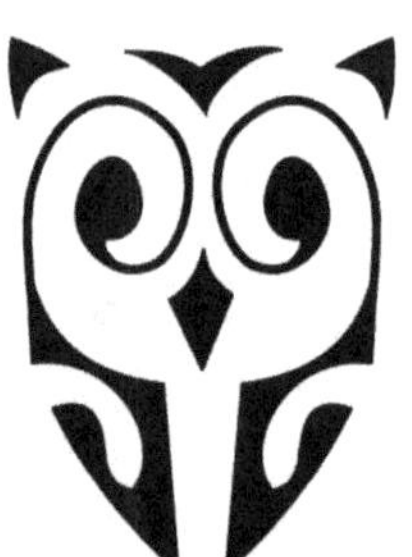

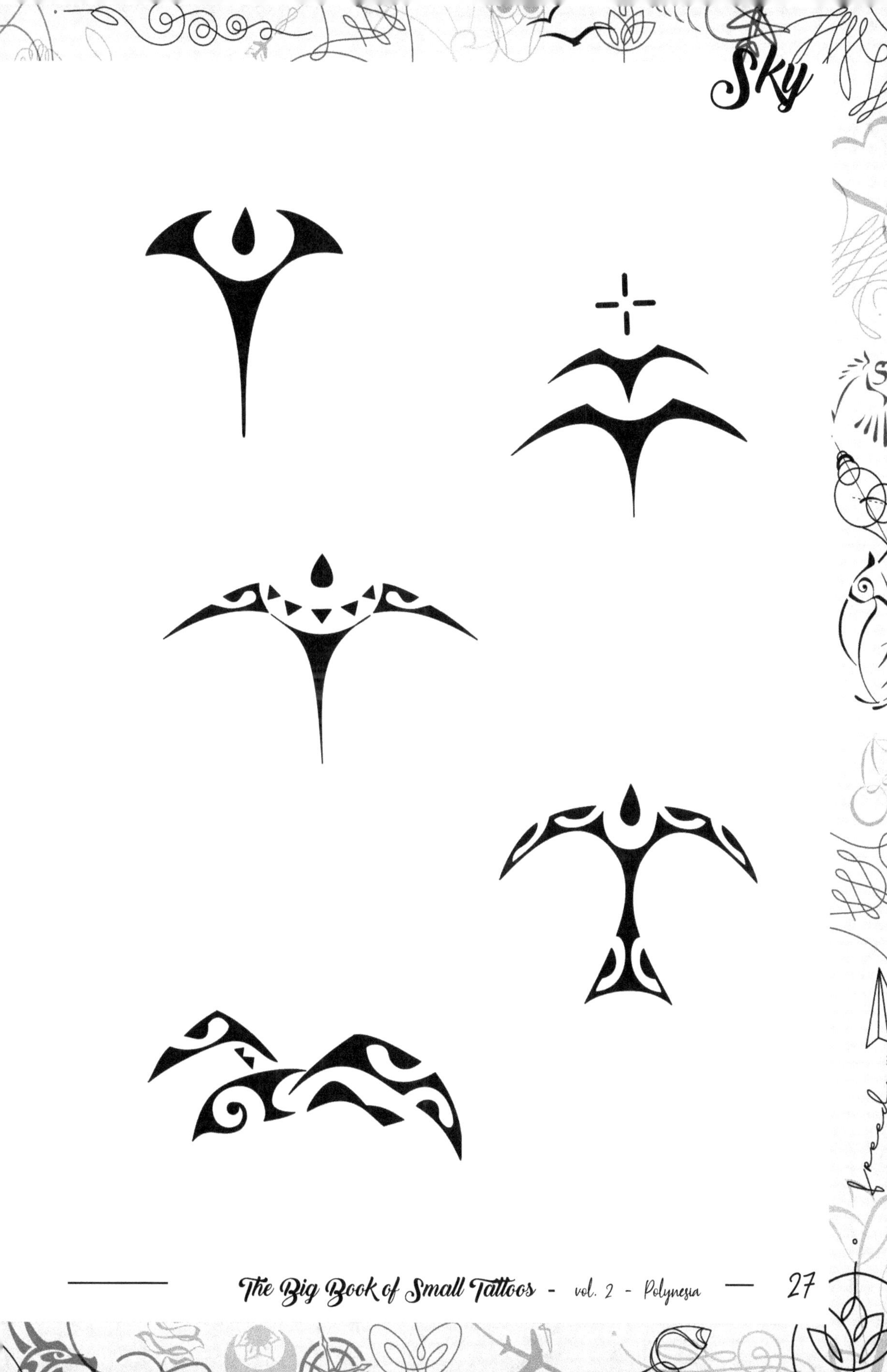

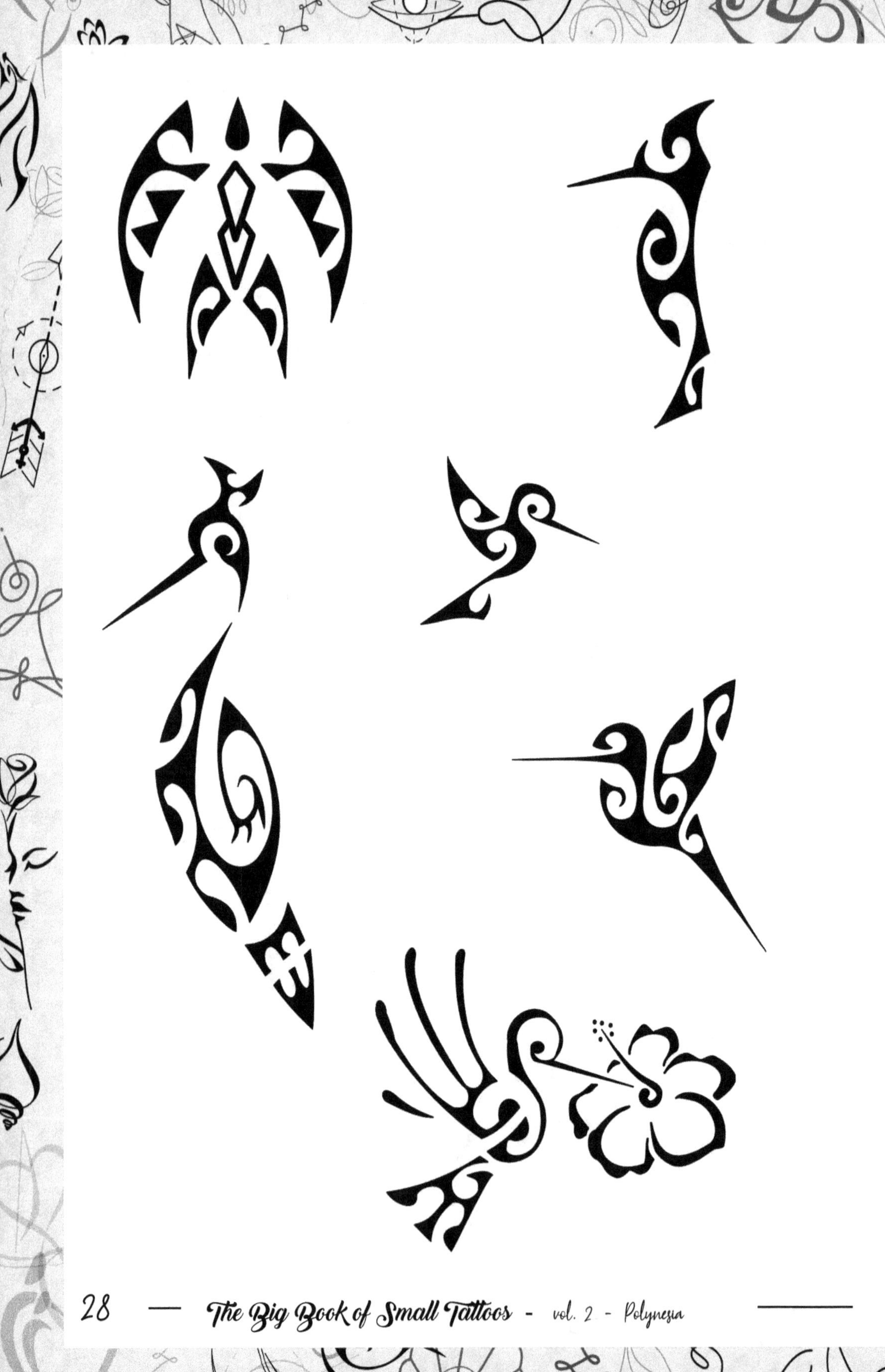

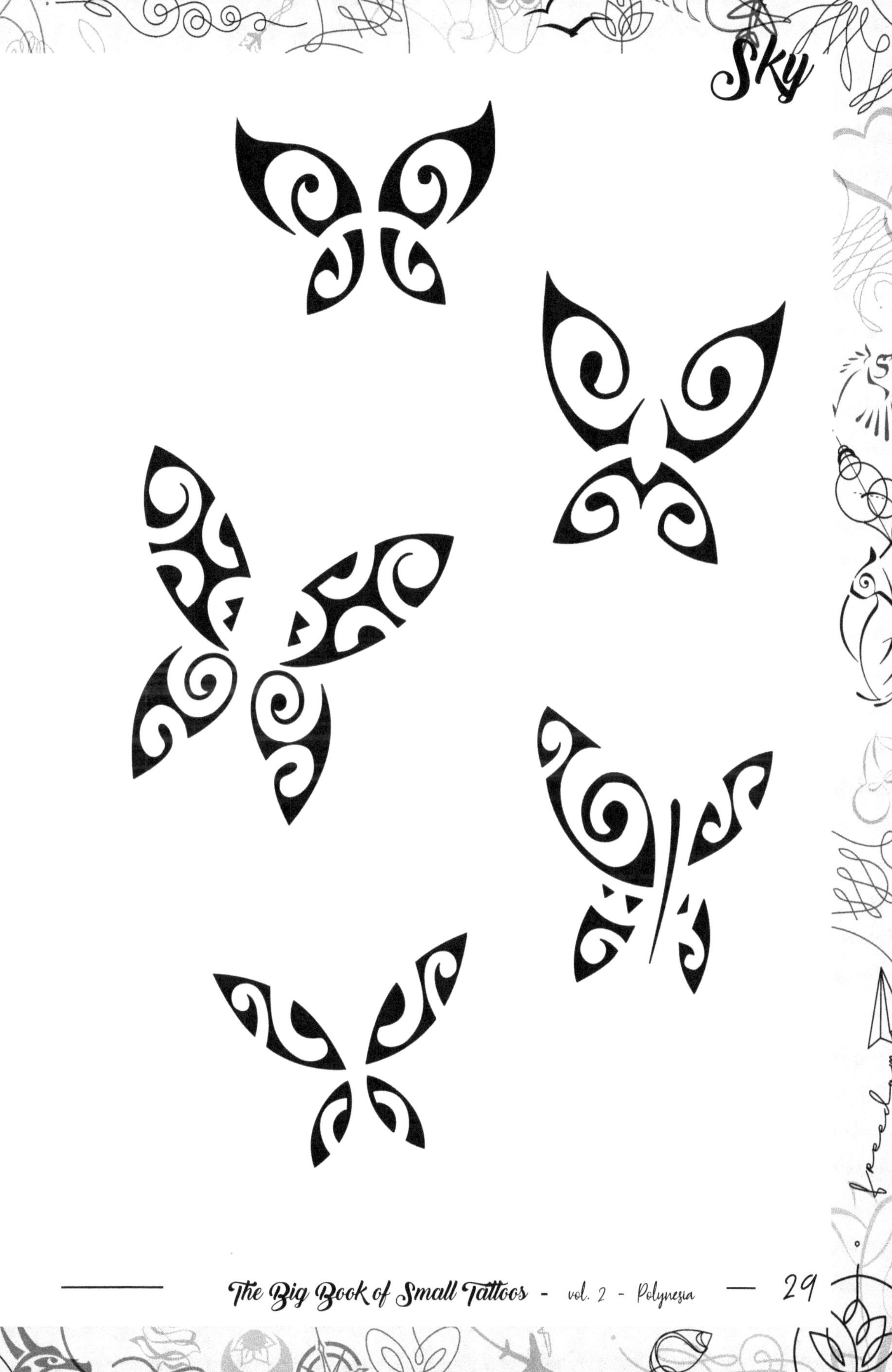

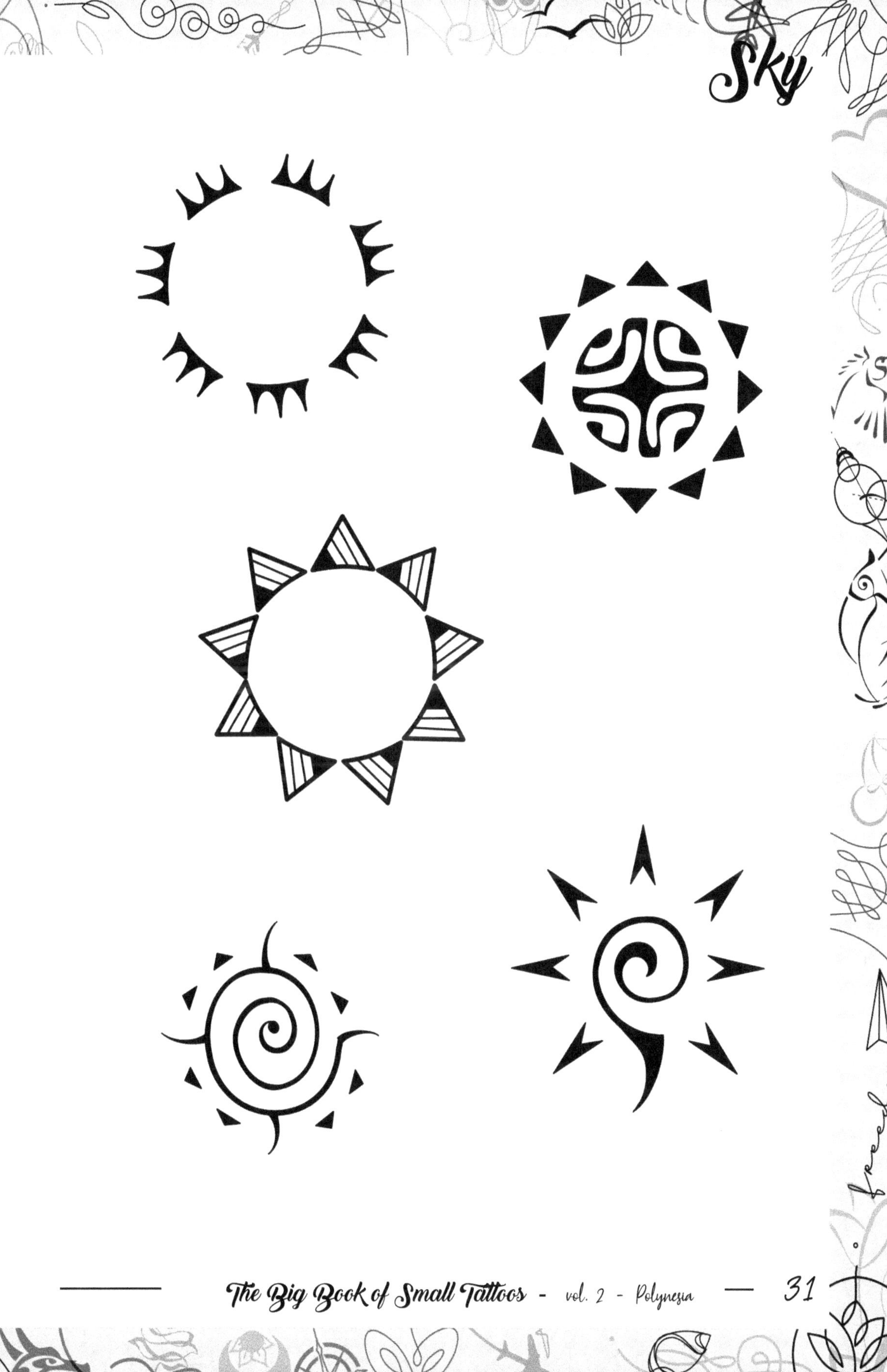

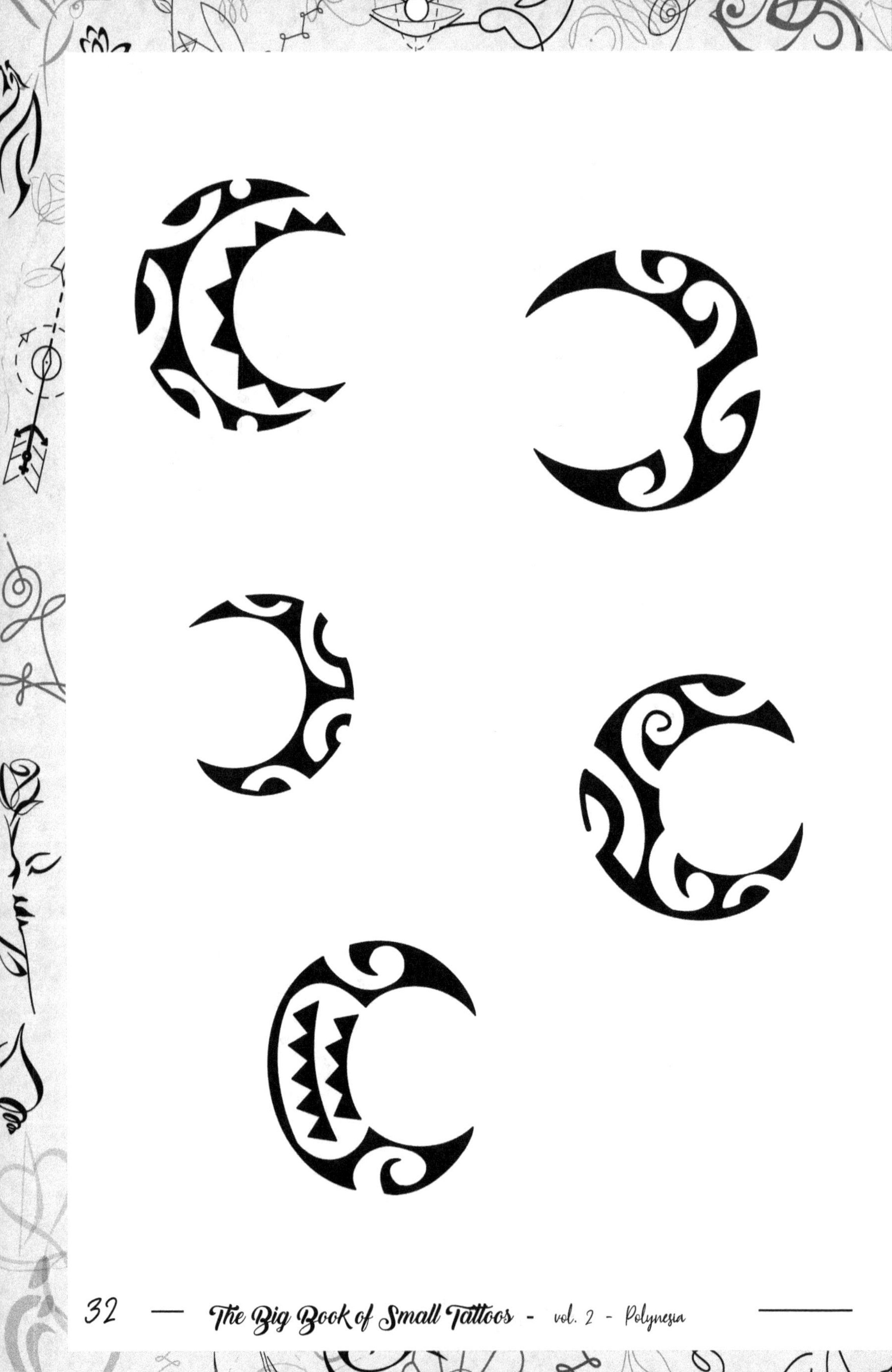

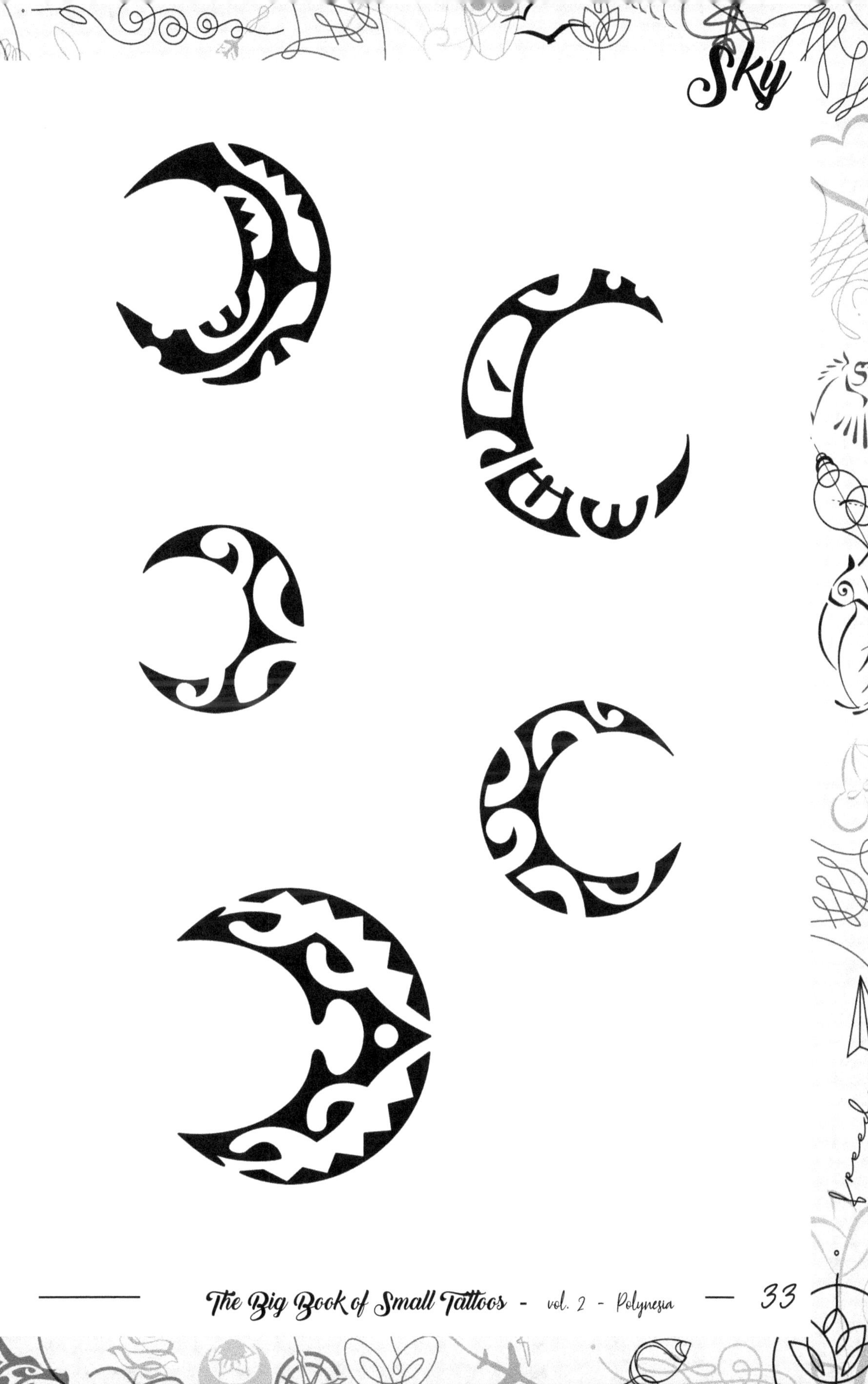

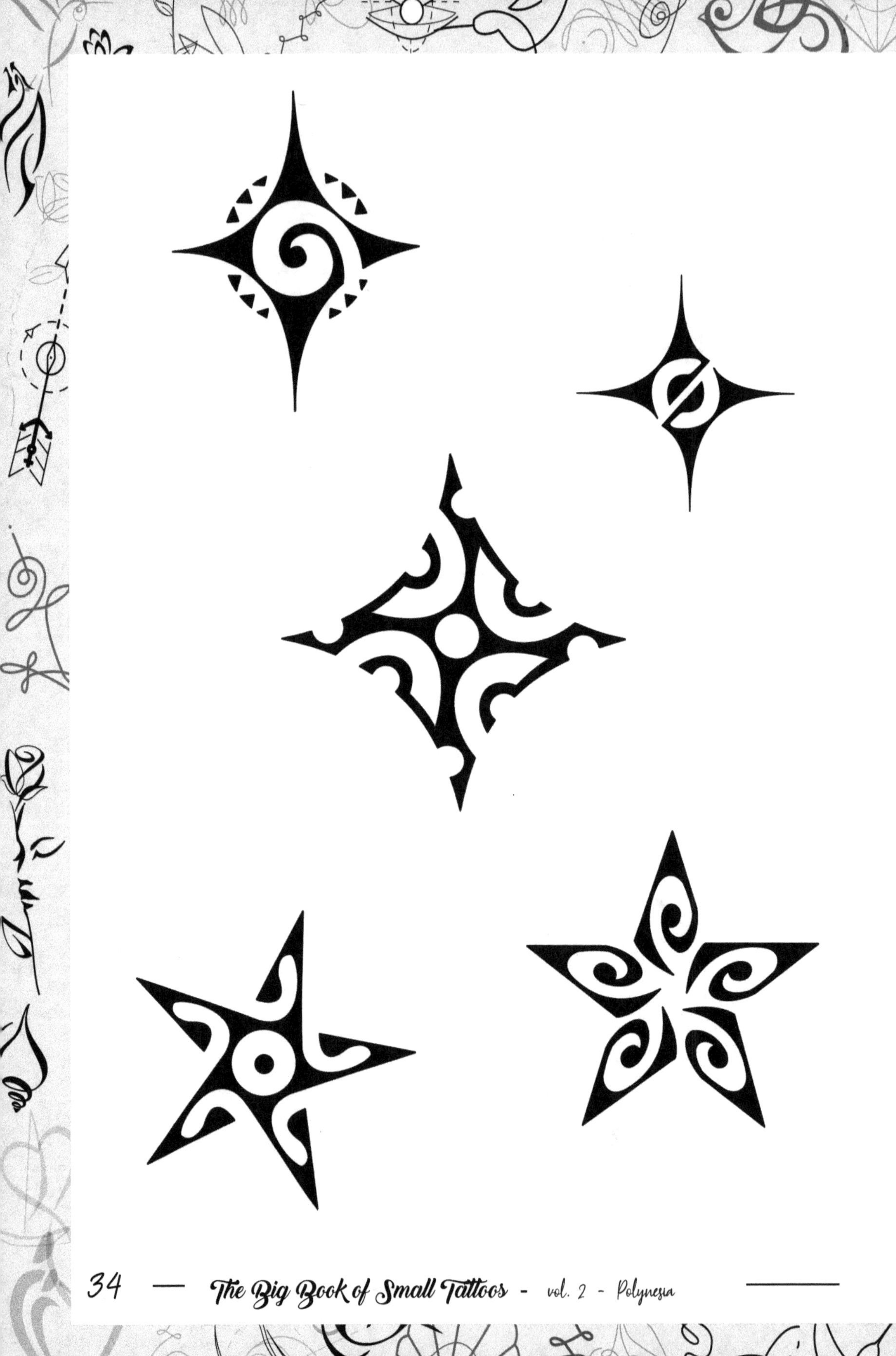

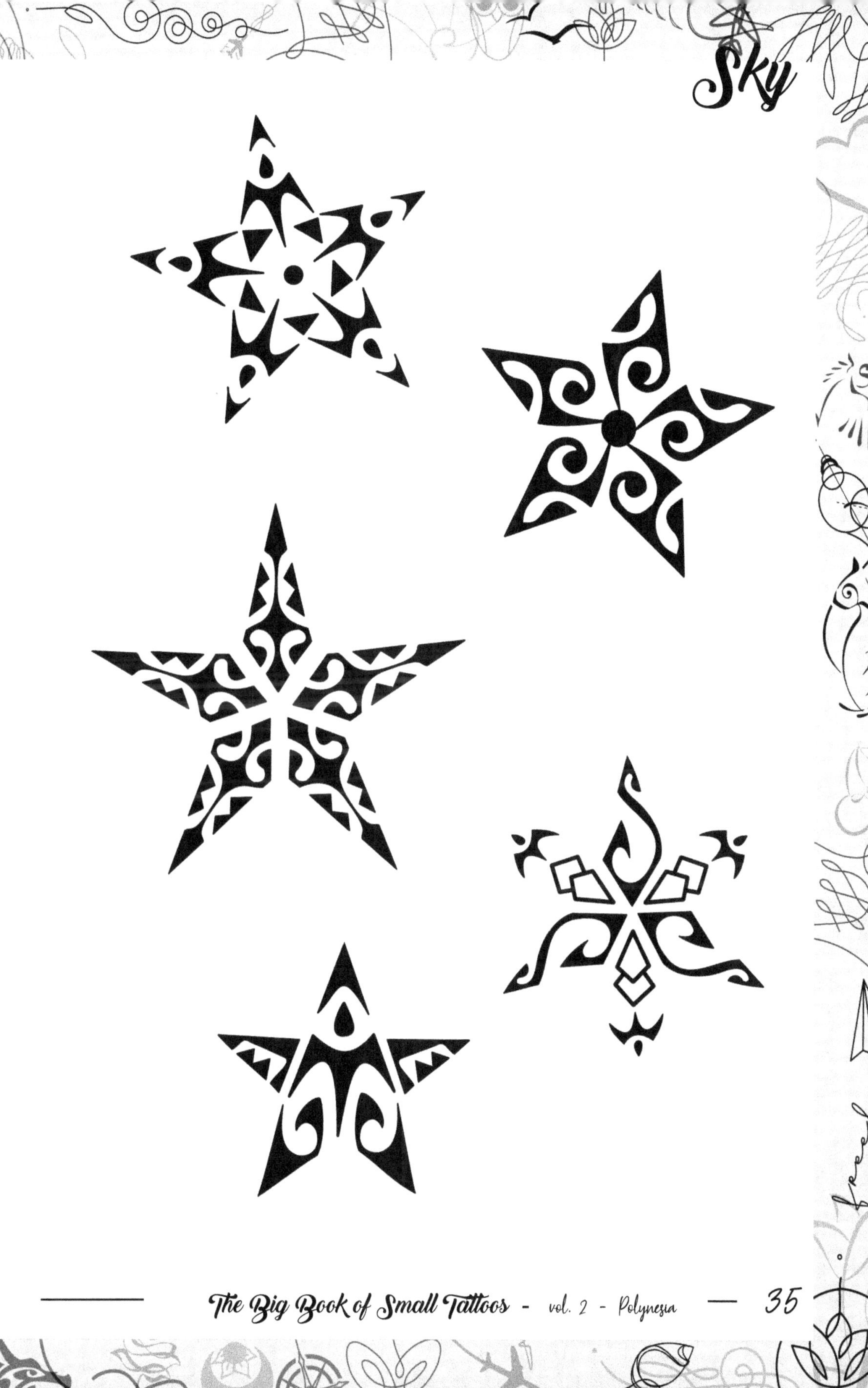

Earth

This section collects designs related to earth, such as flowers, plants, and animals that live on land, like lizards, a frequent presence in Polynesian lore and legends.

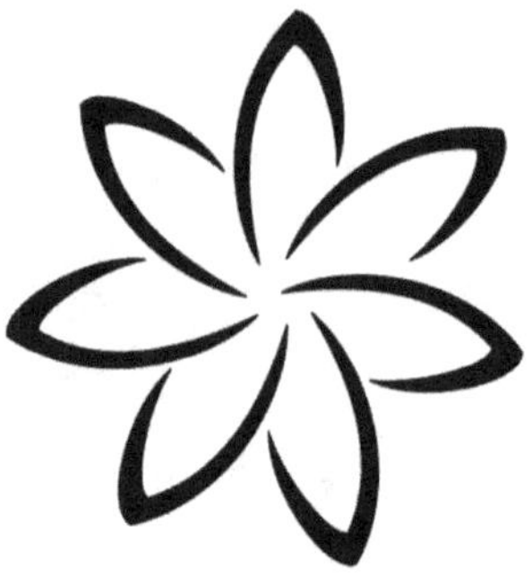

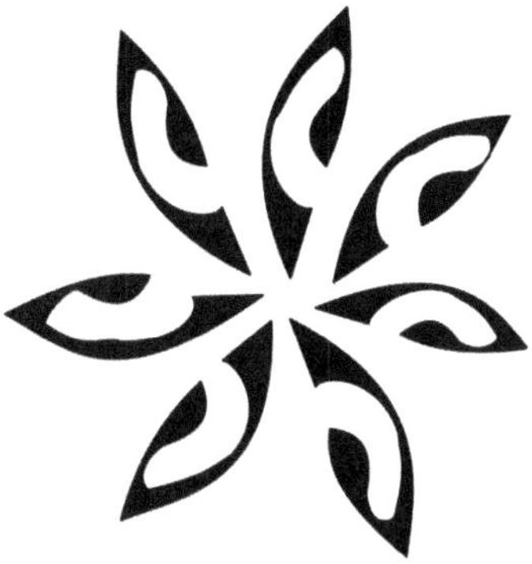

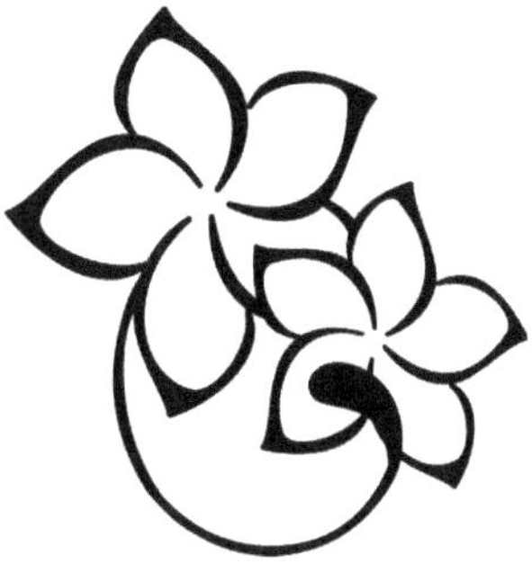

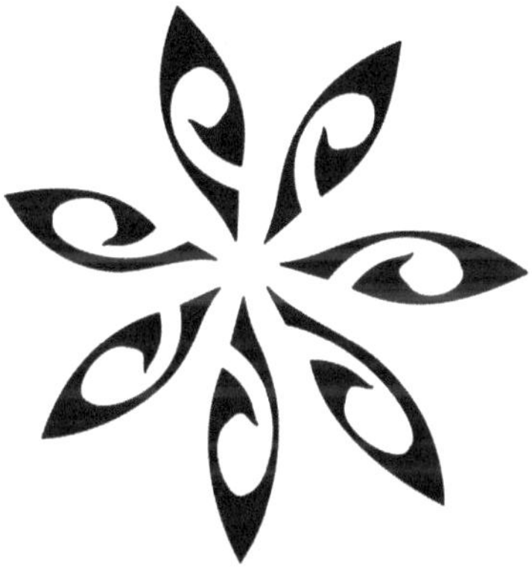

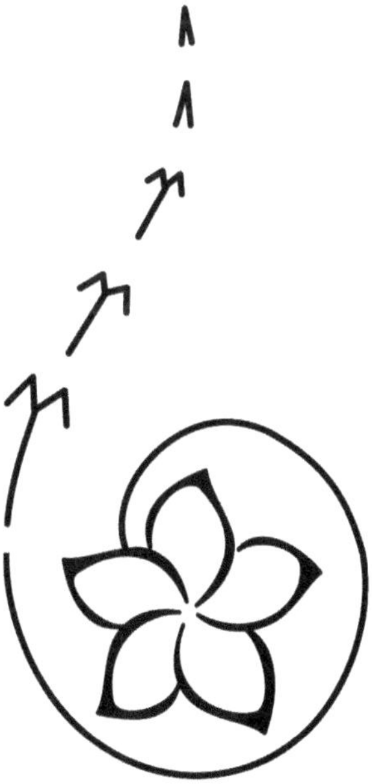

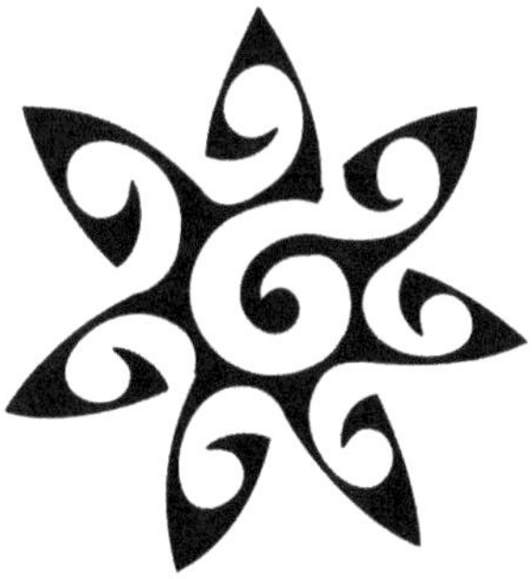

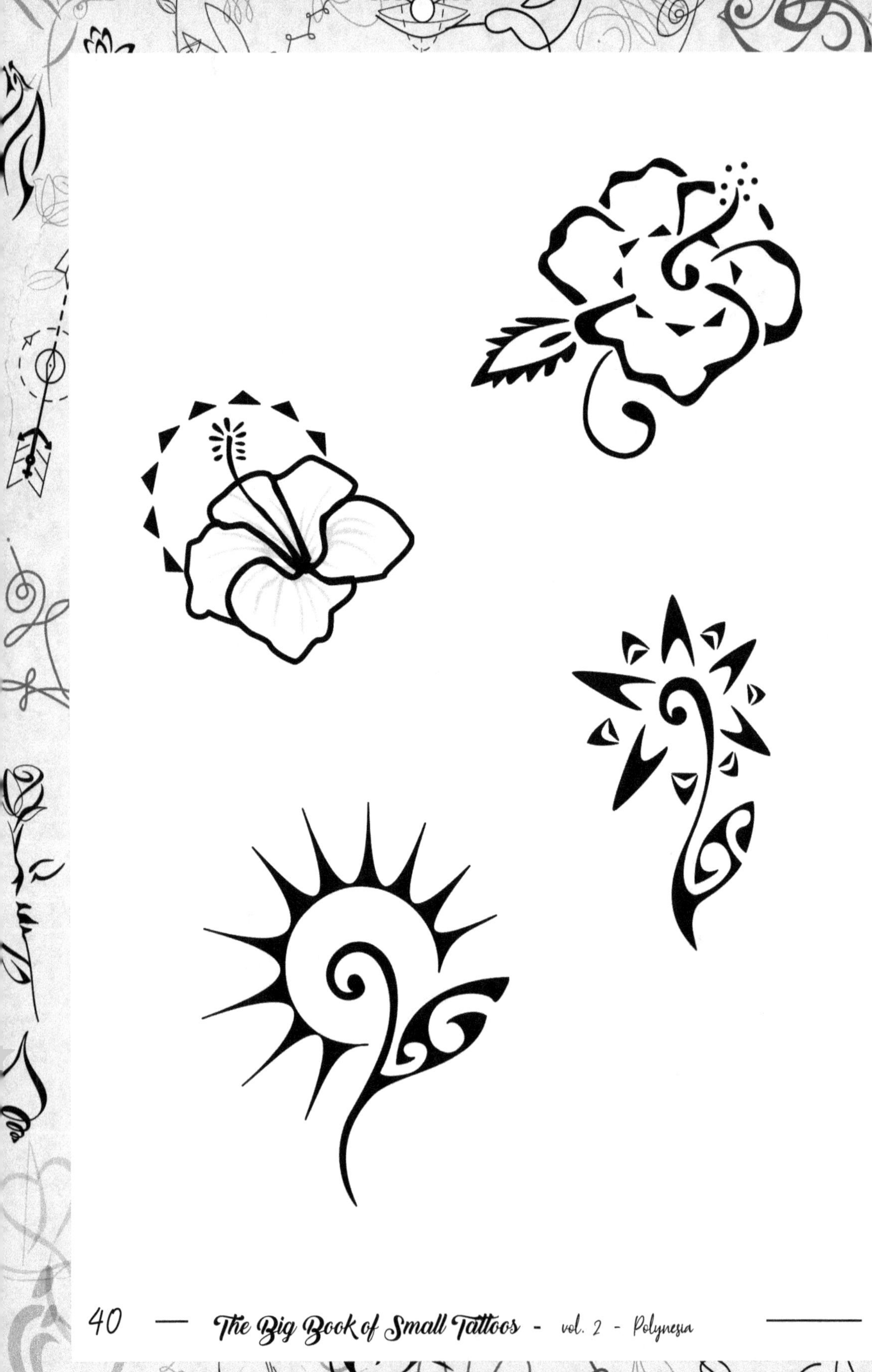

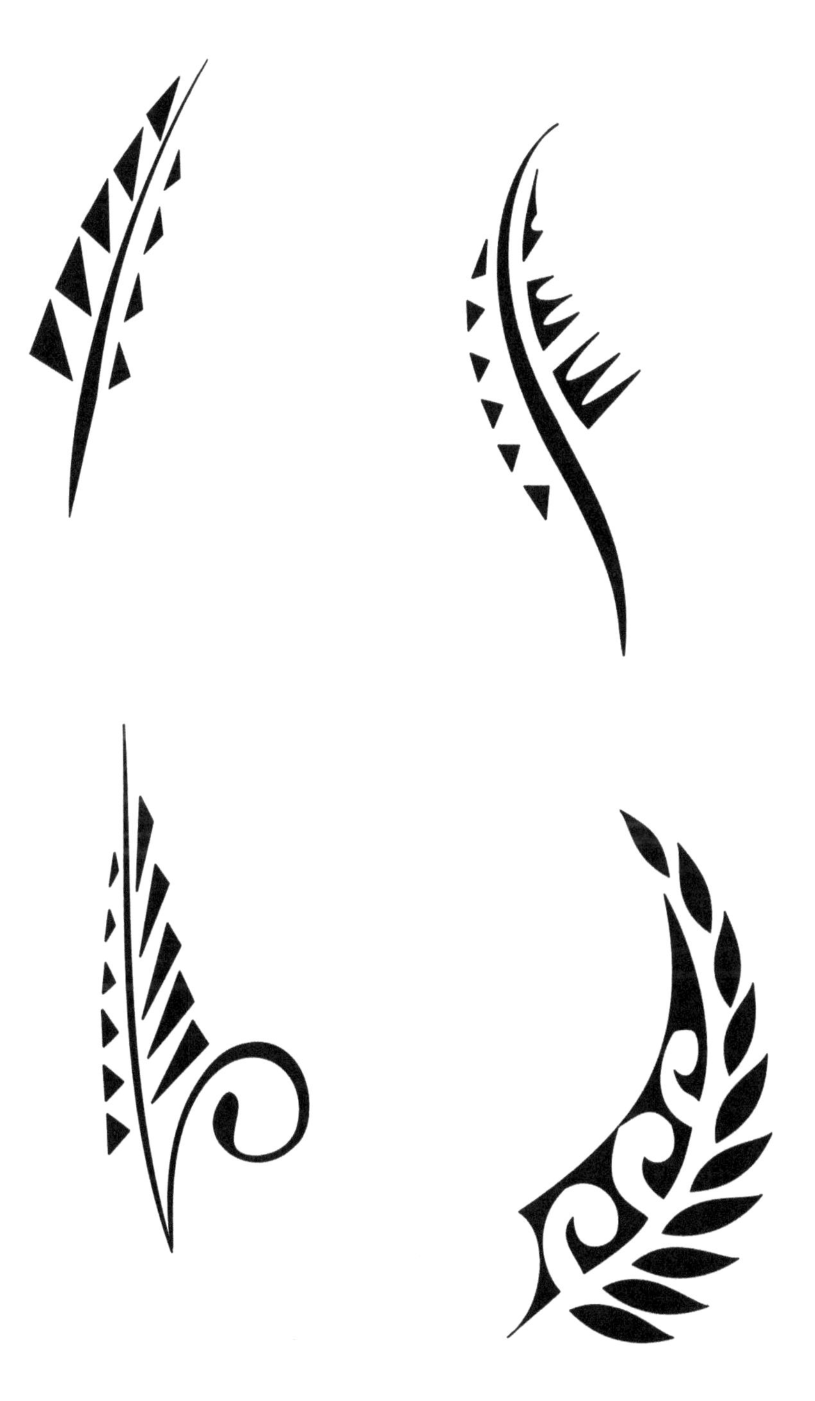

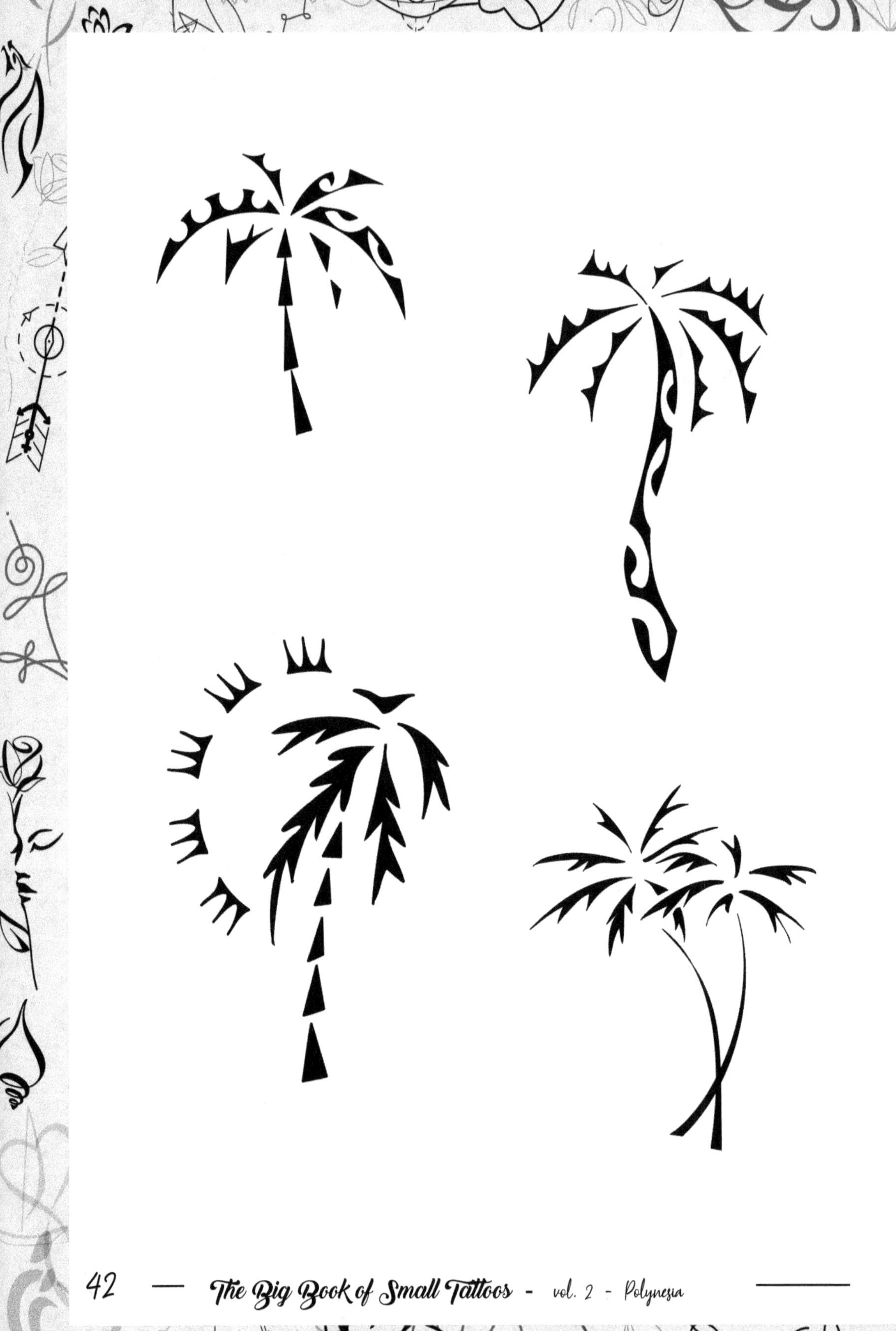

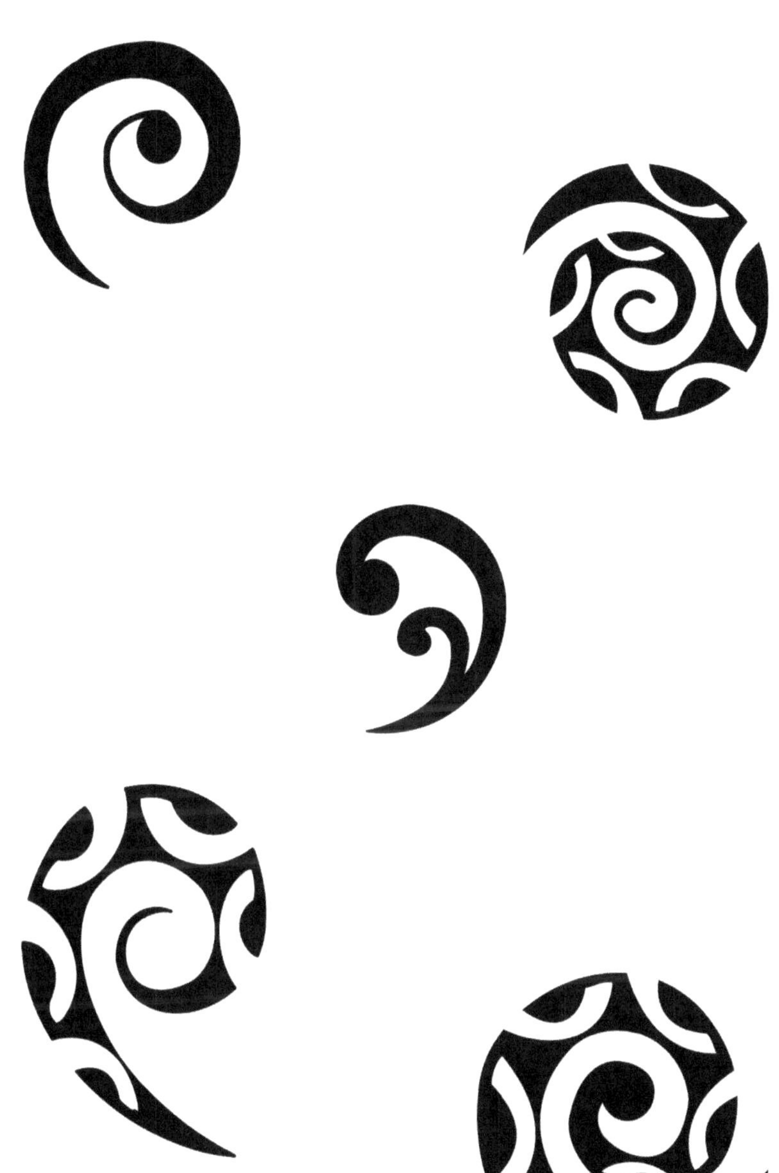

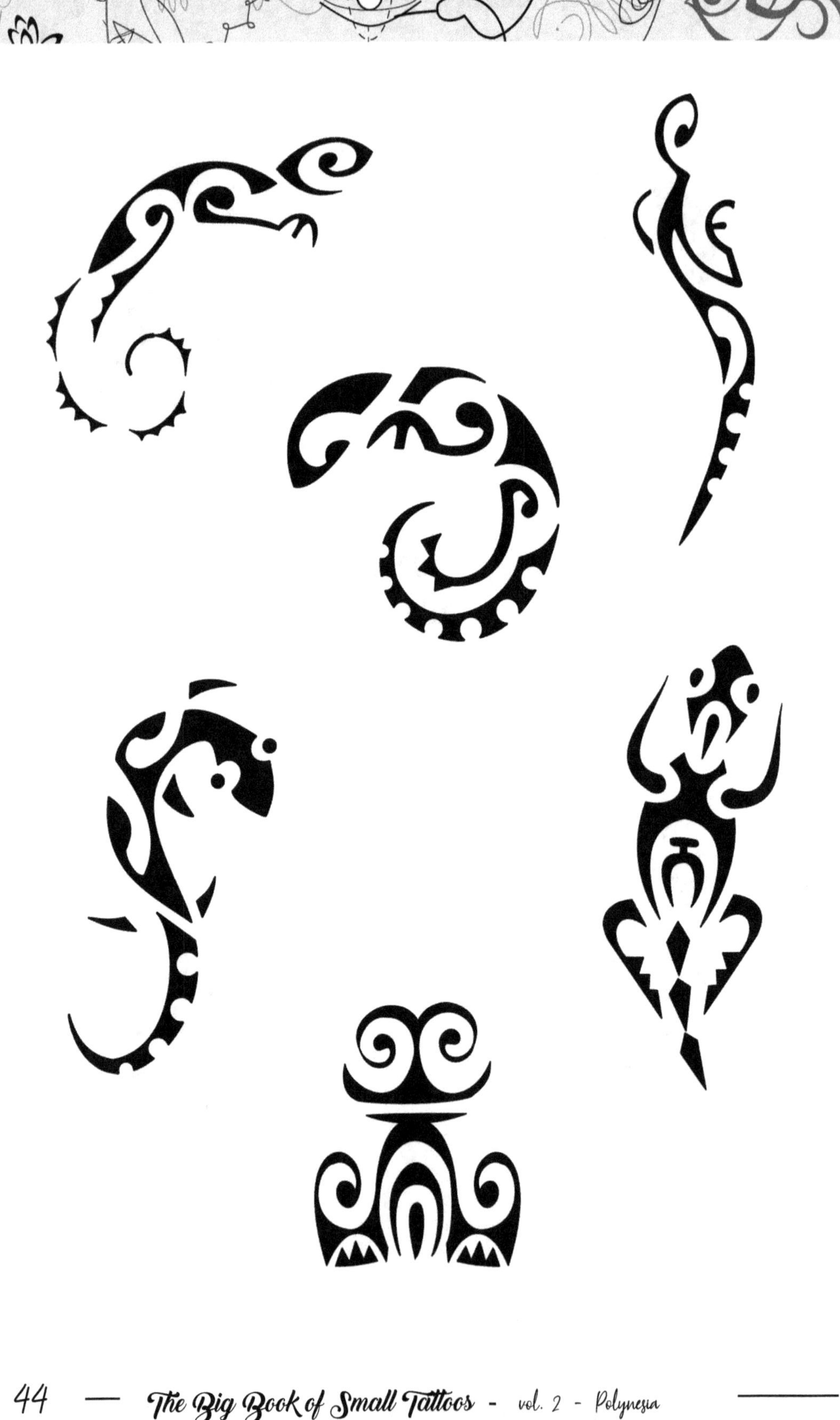

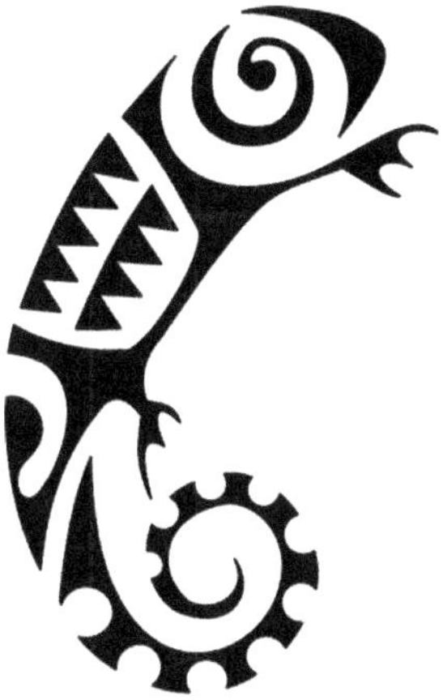

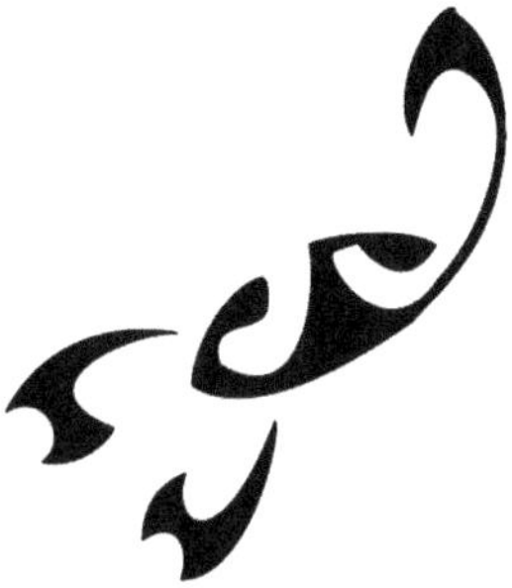

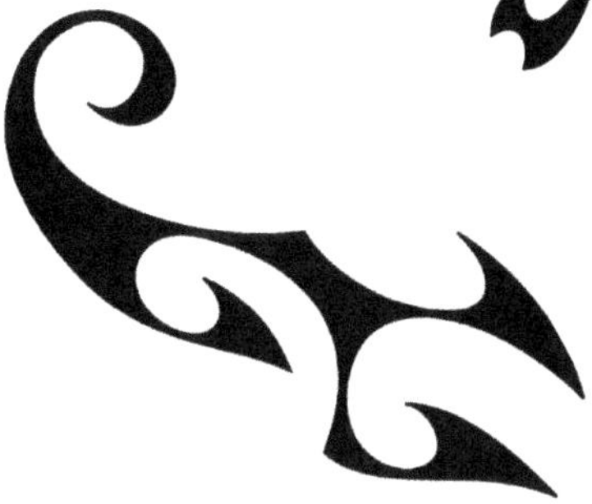

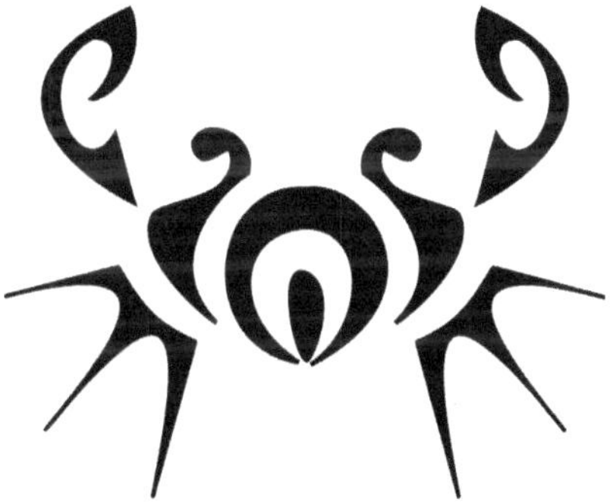

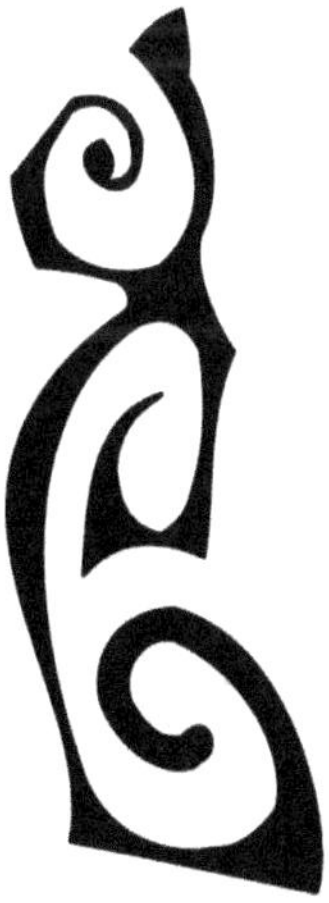

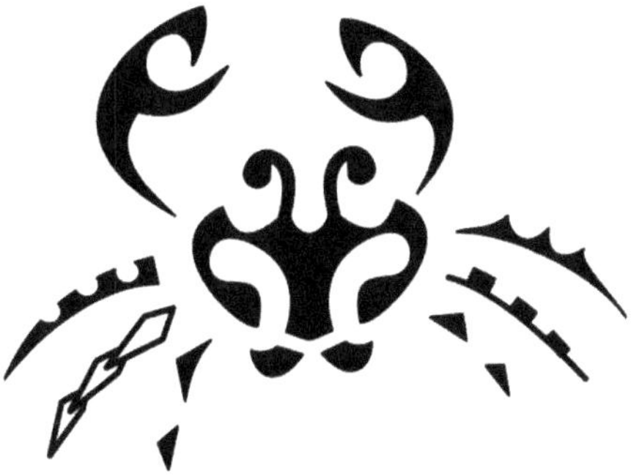

Spiritual world

Polynesian people believed that the key to a healthy and thriving society was finding balance between the world of people, nature, and the world of spirits.

Spirits and deified ancestors can present themselves in many forms, like animals for example, and paying respect to them was a way to earn their favor.

We added a few non-Polynesian symbols to the end of this section, like the Celtic triskell, the heart, and the music clefs, redesigning them in Polynesian style.

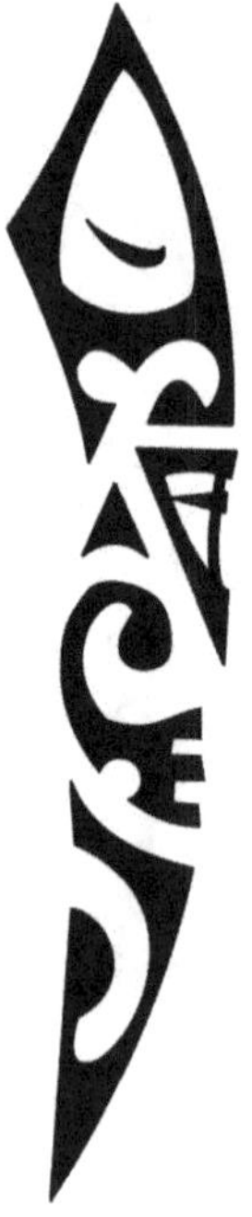

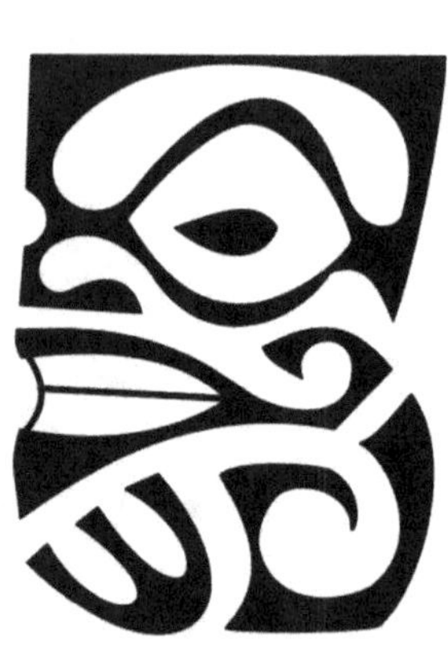

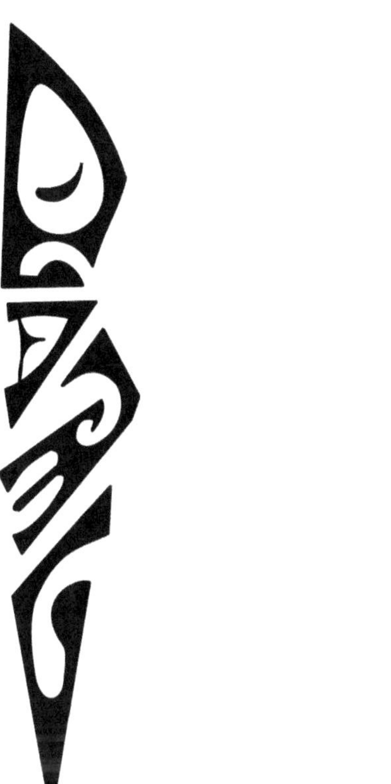

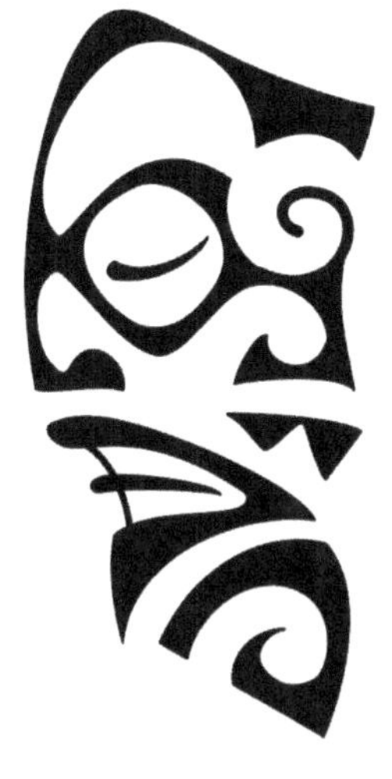

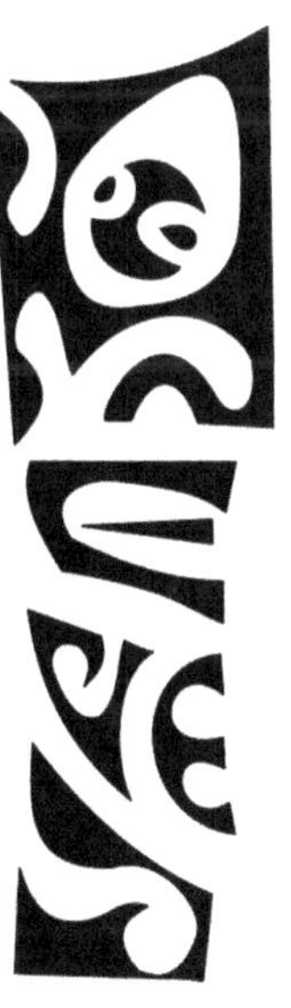

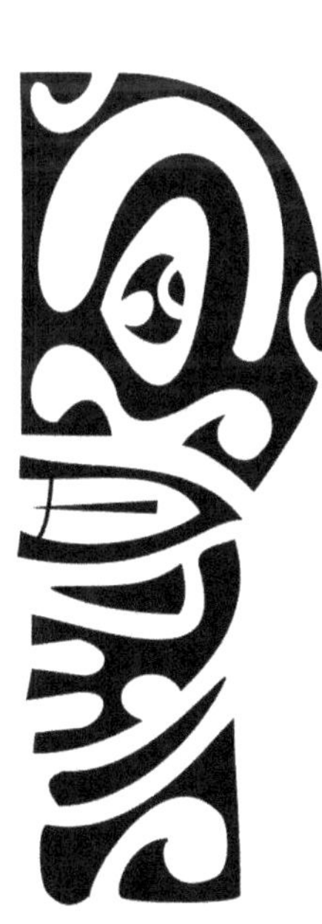

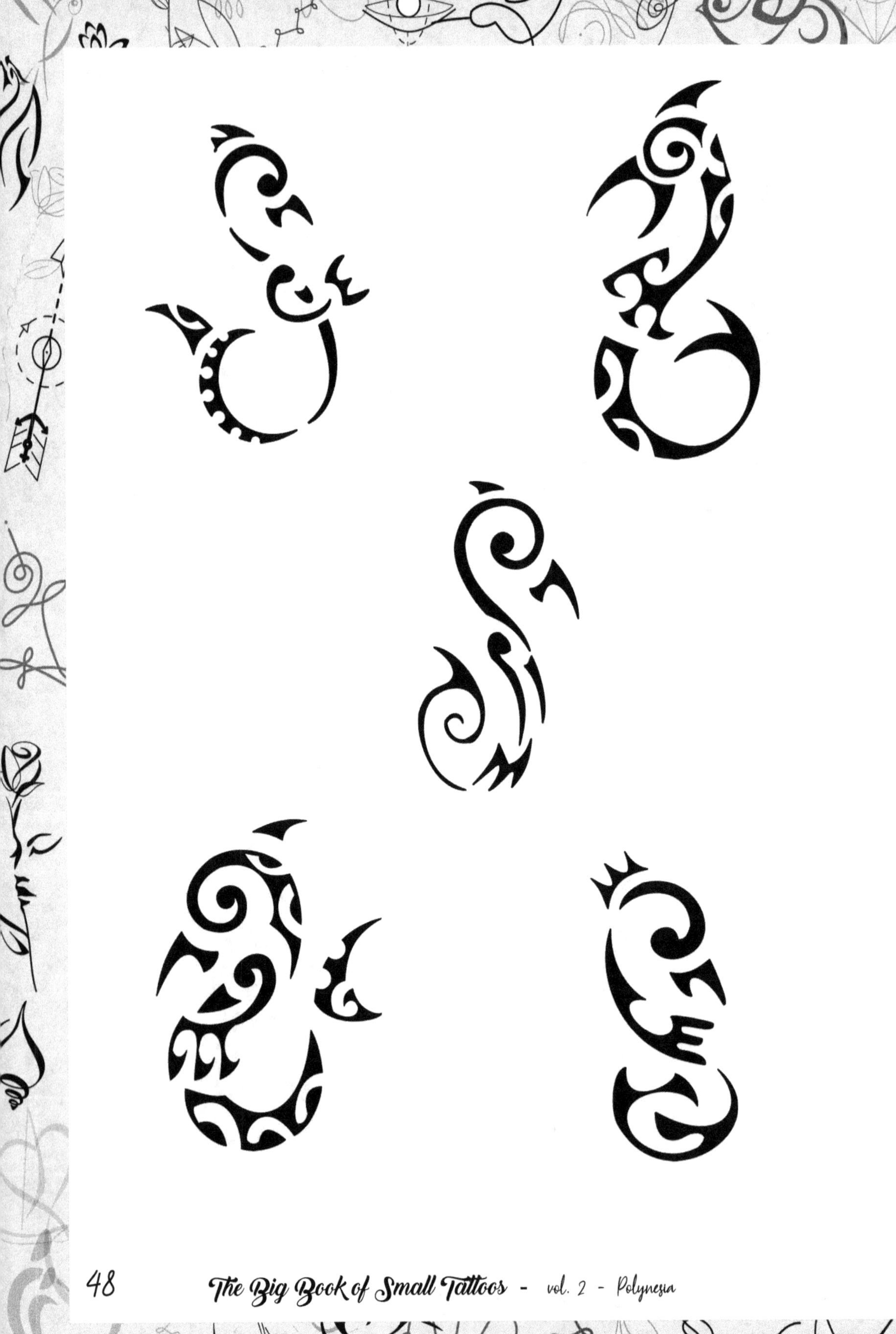

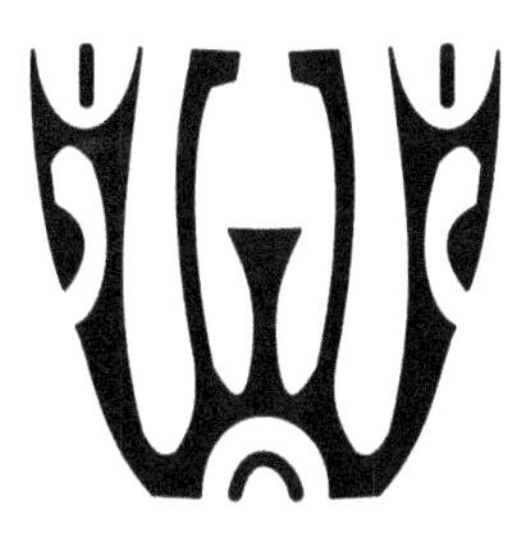

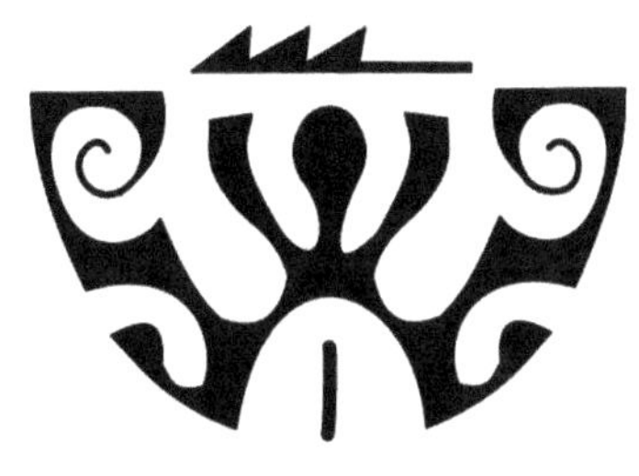

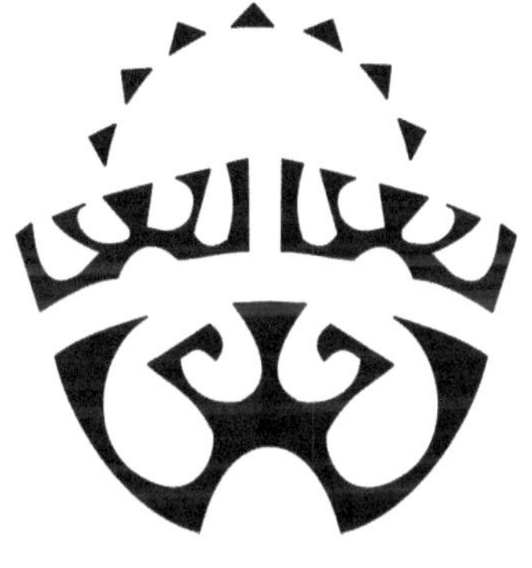

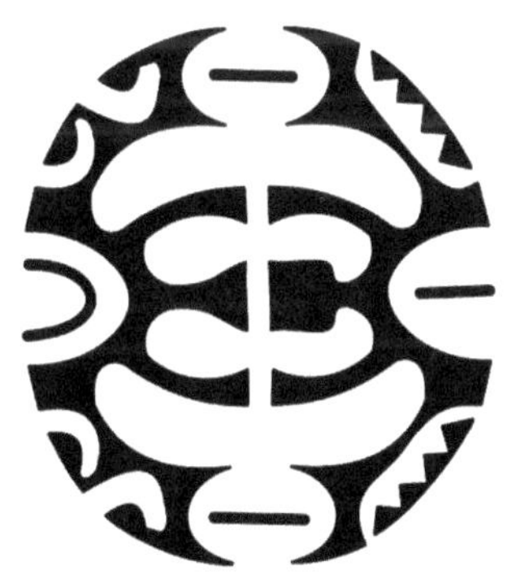

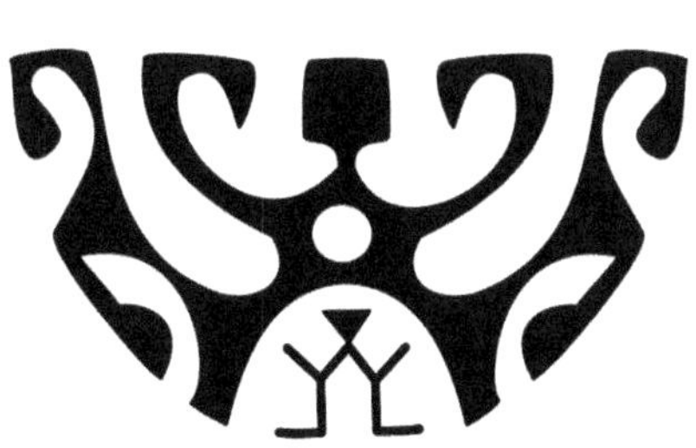

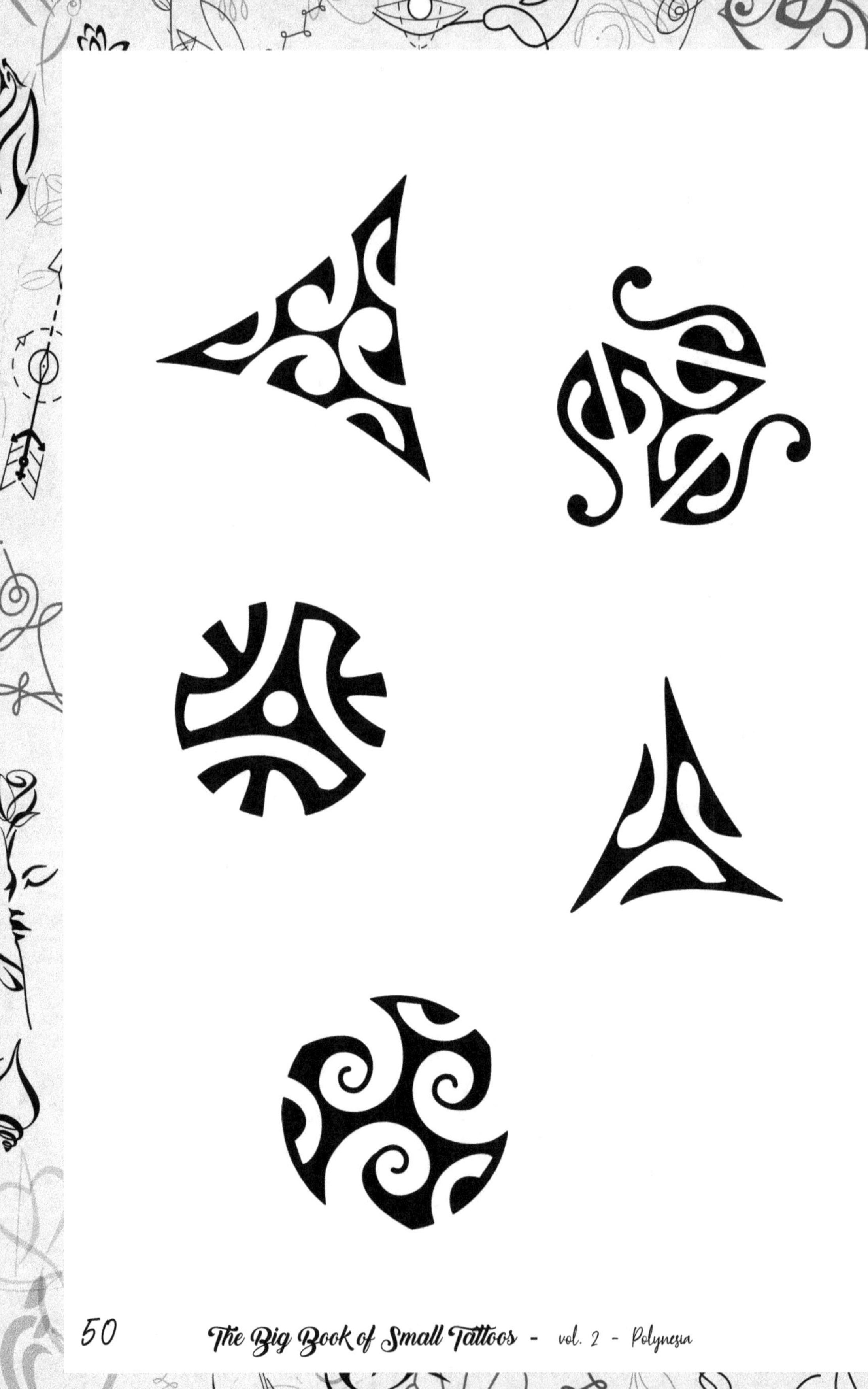

Mixed symbols

The observation of nature allowed Polynesian people to attain incredible feats, like exploring the whole Pacific Ocean with no modern technology by just observing the patterns of waves, currents, winds, clouds, and animal migrations.

This keen attitude for details also allowed them to identify specific characteristics in all sorts of fish, birds, and other animals, which were then used to symbolize those characteristics within their tattoos.

Animals indeed share a great part of the designs in this book, as they played a great part in the life of Polynesian people.

Here are some of the most important, with their associated meanings.

TURTLE

Turtles symbolize voyaging by sea, longevity, and health. They are also one of the main symbols used to represent family.

MANTA

Mantas are majestic animals, whose slow and elegant movements make them appear to be flying underwater. They symbolize beauty and elegance, as well as knowledge and freedom.

SHARK

Polynesian people consider sharks to be strong and adaptable creatures, and regard them as guides for stranded navigators. Hammerhead sharks are a symbol of tenacity and determination, as well as sociality.

DOLPHIN

Dolphins are social animals, among the few that enjoy having play time. They symbolize playfulness, sociability, and joy.

OCTOPUS

The octopus symbolizes adaptability, disguise, smartness, and tenacity.

JELLYFISH

The main meaning of the jellyfish, despite its dangerous side, lies in its calm, effortless way of moving. It symbolizes taking it easy and letting yourself flow along the stream of life without struggling to swim against it.

STARFISH

The starfsh is associated with tenacity and patience, as it's known for moving slow and clinging to the rocks if attacked. The ability to regrow severed limbs makes it a symbol of regeneration, too.

TUNA

Tuna was, and still is, an important source of food for Polynesian people. In tattoos, they symbolize prosperity, abundance, and community.

SWORDFISH

Swordfish symbolize swiftness, determination, and agility in achieving goals.

WHALE

Whales are symbols of abundance and prosperity, as they were a source of food and utensils to the islanders, and they are a symbol of parental love, nurturing, and protection, too.

LIZARD & GECKO

Lizards and geckos are powerful creatures who can bring good luck, communicate with the spirits, and access the invisible world, foreseeing any danger. They are considered guardians and protectors.

FLOWERS

Hibiscus, plumeria, and tiare are the most common flowers in Polynesian designs. Flowers are a constant presence in the nature of Polynesian islands: they symbolize beauty, femininity, grace, sensuality, and joy. They also represent new growth and children.

PALM TREES

Palm trees were sacred to Polynesian people, as they provided them with food, fibers for weaving clothes, roofs to their houses, bowls from coconuts, and wood and leaves for cooking. Soot from burned dry coconuts was used to prepare ink for tattooing.

SEASHELLS

Shellfsh provided Polynesian people with food and utensils made from their shells. They symbolize prosperity, safe shelter, and intimacy, as well as marriage and union if bivalves.

FISH HOOK

Fish hooks are common symbols for plenty, prosperity, abundance, and good luck, as having fish hooks allowed people to tap into the riches of the ocean. They are also used to symbolize knowledge and intelligence (a concept is caught and held like a fish).

ANCHOR

Anchors are symbolic of stability and firmness, going unharmed through the storms of life.

BIRDS

Birds like the tern and the frigate are symbolic of voyages, safe return, and viewing the world from a higher perspective. The hummingbird, who sips nectar from flowers, is regarded as a symbol of taking the best out of life and embodies the spirit of *carpe diem*.

TIKI & MANAIA

A tiki is a representation of a divinity, and it can represent a deified ancestor too. The manaia is a guardian protector shaped with the head of a bird, a human body, and the tail of a fish. It symbolizes balance between the elements and the union of sky, earth, and sea. They are both powerful protective symbols.

SUN

The sun is a universal symbol for life. Polynesian cultures also regard it as a symbol of health, success, joy, and

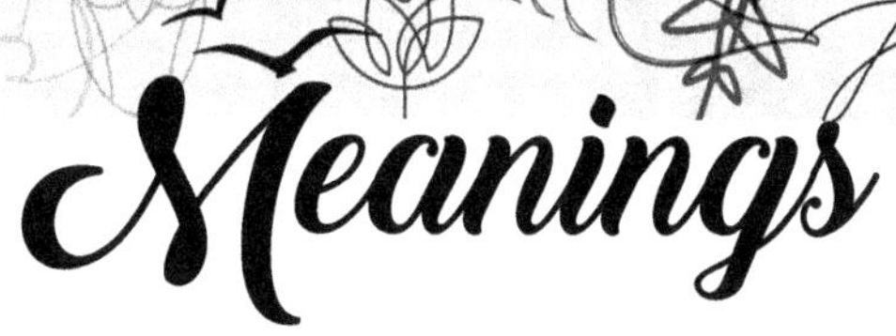

MOON

The feminine counterpart to the sun. It symbolizes feminine energy and fertility. The union of sun and moon, or sunmoon, symbolizes opposites coming together, the impossible that becomes possible.

STARS

Stars represent a fixed point, the direction to be followed, and the goal in front of us to be pursued.

BUTTERFLY & DRAGONFLY

These flying insects symbolize transformation and rebirth. The caterpillar goes through an apparent death, but then is reborn free from earthly bounds. The dragonfly is also a symbol of magic and wonder.

WAVES

Waves remind us of the ocean, of our ancestral cradle where we can still feel at home, safe and nurtured, and they also remind us to respect the sea. They represent change, and also finding stability amidst changes.

CANOE & SAILS

Canoes are symbolic of wanderlust, adventure, and voyages. Sails symbolize freedom, harnessing the power of life's winds to reach to new places.
"It is not the blowing of the wind, but the setting of the sails that will determine our direction in life."—Jim Rohn

All the designs in the books in this series have never been published before; this is a great opportunity to have a tattoo that's one of a kind.

Each small tattoo can be personalized with just a few minor changes, like adding an element, changing the thickness of its lines, or joining two or more designs together.

Adding colors is another great way to personalize them: watercolor style is a perfect match, and it guarantees that there will never be two designs looking the same.

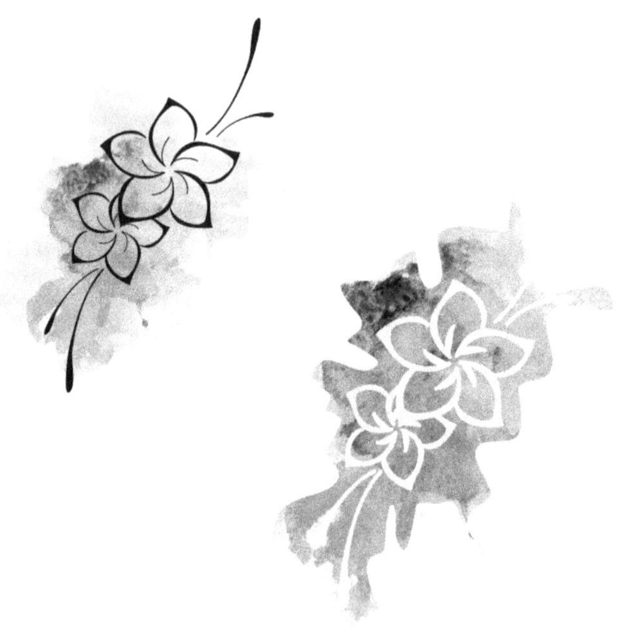

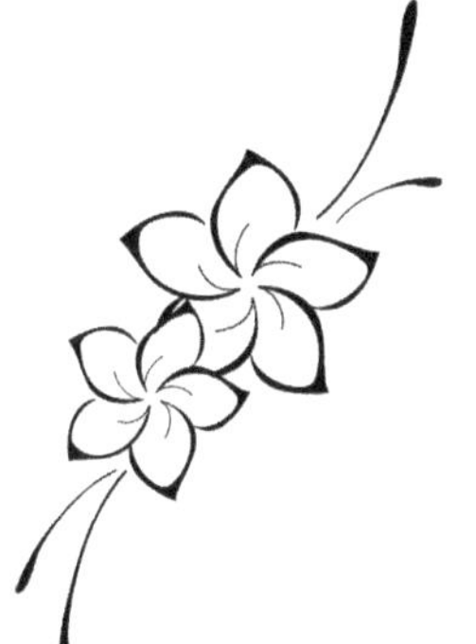

The simplest modification is to thicken some of the lines. It gives more strength and character to a delicate design.

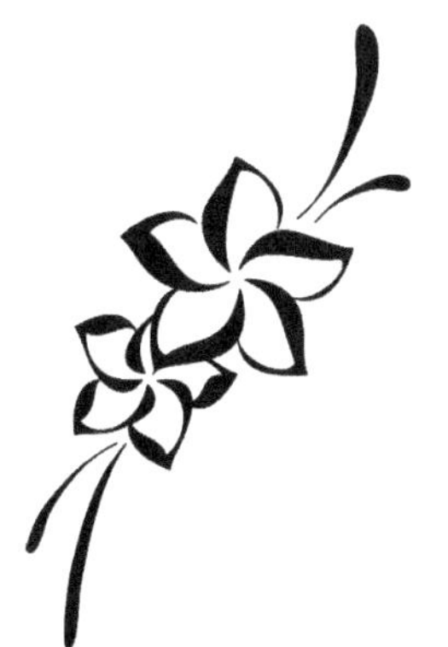

You can also decide to add a shadow to the tattoo, to give it three-dimensionality, or draw it as if it was brush painted. These are all easy ways to make it personal without needing to change the basic symbol.

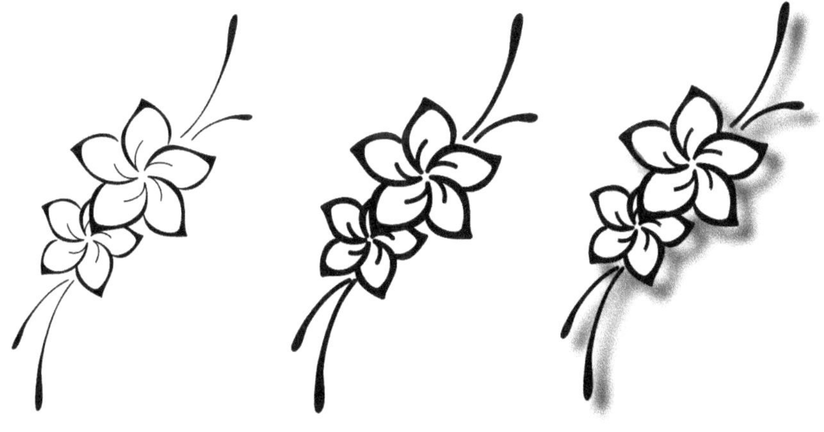

Bonus

The designs in this bonus section come from a free design book featuring 28 protection tattoos. It can be downloaded from www.tattootribes.com

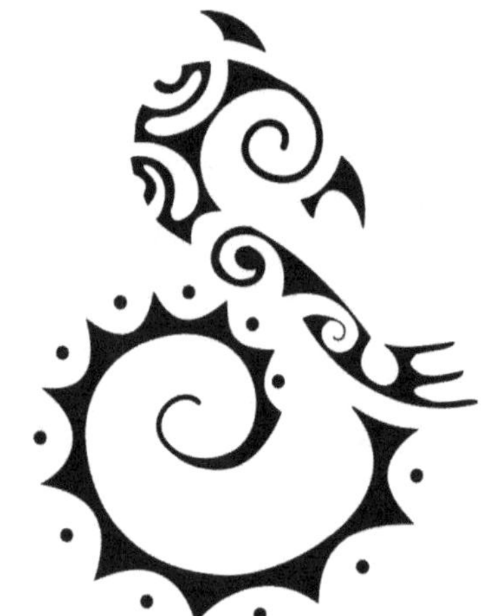

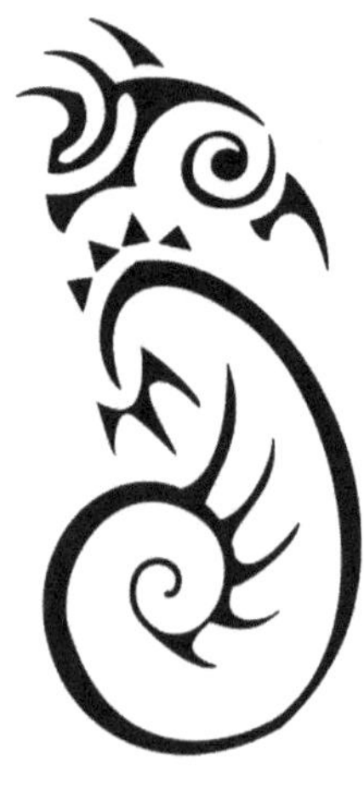

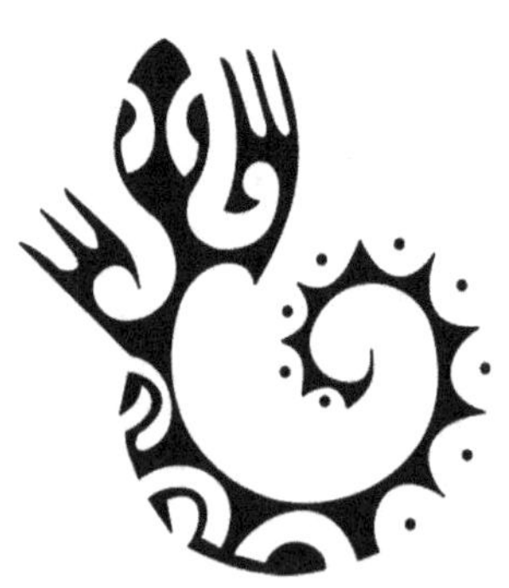

EXTRA BONUS

Follow the QR code on your phone to suggest
new themes you'd like to see in one of the
upcoming books in this series, and if your
suggestion makes it into a book, you'll get
a FREE copy of it!

https://www.small-tattoo-ideas.com/suggest.html  

In the same series:

The Big Book of Small Tattoos - Vol. 0 - Unalome & One-line Tattoos
(2020)
100+ Original Small Tattoos for Women and Men
Can small tattoos be deeply meaningful? The unalome proves it beyond doubt.
Discover 100+ unpublished original unalome and one-line tattoos.

The Big Book of Small Tattoos - Vol. 1 (2019)
400+ Original Small Tattoos for Women and Men
Whether you are approaching tattoos for the first time and want to start small, or
you're a longtime fan and only have just that tiny little spot left, you will appreciate
this book and its philosophy: **small & meaningful**.

More books from TattooTribes:

The Polynesian Tattoo Handbook (2011)
Practical Guide to Creating Meaningful Polynesian Tattoos
Learn Polynesian tattoos and their symbolism. 250+ pages with symbols, their
meanings, their placement on the body, case studies, and step-by-step tattoo
creation, basic elements, and reusable designs.

Polynesian Tattoo Designs (2014)
Vol.1 - Ocean Legacy
A large-format book collecting all 93 Polynesian-styled tattoo designs from design
books numbers 1, 2, 3, and 4, each one accompanied by its stencil: Mantas,
Turtles, Sharks, and Sealife.

The Polynesian Tattoo Handbook, Vol. 2 (2018)
*An In-Depth Study of Polynesian Tattoos and of Their Foundational
Symbols*
Unpacking the five main Polynesian styles: Samoan, Marquesan, Tahitian,
Hawaiian, and Maori. 206 pages, 550+ illustrations, 400+ symbols and variants.

Polynesian Tattoos (2018)
42 Modern Tribal Designs to Color and Explore
A coloring book for adults featuring 42 original tattoos, each one accompanied by a
description of its meanings.

TattooTribes.com
2021